In Your Face!

In Your Face!

Sports for Love and Money

Lee Ballinger

VANGUARD BOOKS   CHICAGO

Published by Vanguard Books, Inc.
P. O. Box 3566, Chicago, IL 60654
ISBN 0-917702-12-3
Printed in the United States of America

Cover photo by Martin J. Masel.

To Erica and Jesse Joe

Acknowledgements

I would like to express my deep appreciation to all those who took the time and trouble to read and comment on the manuscript as it wound its way to completion. While I take sole responsibility for the ideas expressed in the book, it would not exist without the help and guidance of many others.

I would particularly like to thank the staff of Vanguard Books who worked so hard with me to see this book through because they understood the importance of what the book has to say. The professional expertise and deep social understanding of my editor, Arlee Frantz, were indispensable in clearly crystallizing my thoughts on the printed page. Sheridan Talbott has spared no effort to design and implement a promotional effort which will, hopefully, insure that this book reaches the wide audience for which it was intended. Without Sheridan's hard work and unflagging enthusiasm, it is doubtful that this book would have seen the light of day.

Finally, thanks to my late father, a champion high school athlete who tried to steer me right by putting his ass on the line time and time again. After fighting my way through a war and a couple of recessions, I think I finally understand what he was talking about.

Table of Contents

Introduction

I wrote this book because I'm mad as hell about what's being done to sports in the United States. Everything is being subordinated to the drive for maximum profit. The World Series is played in a winter rainstorm. Our high schools produce illiterate graduates who, if they have a good jump shot, are used and then discarded by the colleges. The increase in women's participation is turned into new industries like the "jogbra." Everything from powerlifting championships to the U.S. Olympic teams to Puerto Rican youth baseball is owned by some corporation. The discrimination against minorities, which means an annual $36 billion dollar bonus to U.S. industry, is a way of life in sports. It may soon be cheaper to put on a wedding than to take your family to a pro football game. Northern states try to compete with the Sunbelt by giving tax breaks to industry while their eroding tax base results in the elimination of athletic programs and even entire school systems. The NCAA is on the verge of eliminating scholarships for all sports that do not provide them and the networks with a profit.

The corporate and financial interests that have taken over sports and run them without regard to the people involved are the same interests which gouge us at the gas pump and send out plant-closing announcements while we sleep. Gyms are padlocked while military contractors are given the key to the public treasury. The steel mill where I work has no recreational facilities and pollutes the air so badly that it is unsafe to go outside and exercise anywhere in the entire valley. It might even be shut down by the time you read this, which will mean no more money for sports where my children go to school.

Let's face facts. My generation grew up during the post-World War II period when the economy was ever-expanding. The majority of us took for granted opportunities in sports as both a participant and a spectator. But now the world economy is violently contracting and our children no longer have easy access to organized sports for exercise and recreation, something we thought was as much a part of life as earth, wind, or fire.

As long as we allow sports to function primarily as a tax shelter or "attractive investment," the deterioration will continue. Maximum profit means minimum opportunity. Miller Beer or Adidas or ABC-TV doesn't care about sports or about you and me. They are interested only in the bottom line.

I didn't write this book just to be a fly in the ointment. It isn't intended as "interesting commentary" to be left on coffee tables. I wrote it as a weapon that can be used to clarify the real situation in sports and to indicate what we can do about it.

I suspect that you are as mad as I am and I hope that you will join with me and millions of others so that the necessary changes can be made.

Lee Ballinger
January 1981

The Owners: Figures Don't Lie But Liars Can Figure

Seldom since the days of the Third Reich has there been such an effective use of the "Big Lie" as there is today regarding the finances of professional sports. Everything you think you know about who is getting over and who isn't is completely wrong.

The Owner: Just a Wild and Crazy Guy?

The owner of a professional sports franchise: what a delightful, wacky guy! Even though he knows he'll lose money, he sinks millions into the team. Forced to the wall by his greedy, ungrateful players, he throws away even more money "to keep baseball in my favorite city" or "to remain competitive." Why does he do it? Is he just on an ego trip? A frustrated jock? A gloryhound?

The truth is that all owners today are either corporations or part-owners of corporations. Living in the United States should have taught us all at least one thing: corporations, and the people who own them, never ever do anything for fun, as a hobby, or because they love a city. The George Steinbrenners of this world have the same goal as Exxon, General Motors, or U.S. Steel: maximum profit.

Yankee owner Steinbrenner makes a fortune through his control of American Shipbuilding. But when it comes to the ball team he is portrayed in the media as a mad spendthrift. Millions for Catfish Hunter, Luis Tiant, Reggie Jackson, Bob Watson, Gaylord Perry. This guy is willing to go out and lose his shirt just for the thrill of being part of a champion. Oh yeah? In 1978 the Yankees took in more than $13 million at the gate and at least $3 million in broadcast rights, advertising, and other income. When Steinbrenner was asked if it were true that the Yankees made a clear profit of $2 million that year, he replied, "I'd rather not comment on that but let's say the last two years have been profitable."[1]

The Yankees are not alone. The few facts that filter out from behind the owners' iron curtain tell a story quite different from the one on the sports page. In 1977 the Cincinnati Reds made a gross profit of $6.7 million after they raised ticket prices twice in three years. Miami Dolphins' owner Joe Robbie was a two-bit lawyer from Minneapolis when he created the team with a $100,000 investment. Today he is the majority owner of a $20 million property. In 1978 the Green Bay Packers reported a 700 percent increase in profits in one year, and they have the lowest ticket prices in the league. Between 1950 and 1977 major league baseball's concession revenues rose 2,552 percent. The NFL Constitution prohibits any nonprofit organization from owning a franchise.

If the owners really want to convince us of their poverty, why don't they make their financial records public? In 1956 the Red Sox told *The Sporting News* that they had lost $616,000 the previous year. At a Congressional hearing they were forced to admit that they had actually turned a profit of $122,000.

There is no evidence that the owners take the Ninth Commandment any more seriously today. For example, Toronto Maple Leafs' owner Harold Ballard did a year in prison after conviction on 47 counts of fraud and theft of team funds.

Doesn't it seem strange that so many millionaires and corporations are standing in line to buy teams if they're such a bad investment? Jerry Buss, owner of the Los Angeles Lakers, didn't mind the wait and here's why: "The Lakers are a good ordinary investment. In the past, they have probably averaged around $500,000 a year in operational profits, and the franchise value has appreciated $500,000 a year. You could get the same return with high quality bonds. However, if we get some pay television there, that could add as much as $2.5 million in profits."[2]

The fact of the matter is that it isn't the players who are pampered. It's the owners. Let us count the ways.

Tax Breaks

The special tax breaks the team owners receive are the most important factor in the profitability of professional sports. They are the clue that solves the crime and enables us to understand why there is such a corporate hunger for ownership of sports franchises. The following explanation is a little complicated. But once it's understood, we'll all be able to argue with George Steinbrenner if he comes into the corner bar to talk to "ordinary people" as he claims he likes to do.

The bulk of the value of a professional sports franchise is in the player contracts, the pieces of paper which legally bind the players to the team. What else is there? A few desks and chairs in an office, a roomful of equipment, and that's about it.

In the mysterious language of accounting, player contracts are known as "capital assets of the enterprise." No other industry in the United States is allowed to treat its employee contracts as capital assets. The best thing about a capital asset is that it is depreciable. This means that its value can be subtracted from the actual profits of an individual or corporation before taxes are figured. It was due in large part to depreciation that 250 millionaires paid no taxes in 1978.

Let's work out an example. Suppose you are one of the new owners of the New York Knicks, which your syndicate bought for $2 million. You claim $1,500,000 of that purchase price as the value of the player contracts and depreciate it over five years. You will then be entitled to a $300,000 annual deduction ($1.5 million divided by five). If the net profit *before depreciation* is $100,000, you will subtract your $300,000 depreciation deduction and just like magic your profit becomes a $200,000 loss. If your income from other sources places you in the 70 percent tax bracket (and if it didn't, you could not afford a franchise), every dollar of this "loss" will reduce your tax liability by 70 cents. The $200,000 loss will mean tax relief of $140,000. Thus you and your fellow owners will realize a $100,000 profit plus tax relief of $140,000 for a total cash-flow benefit from the team of $240,000. The team shows a bookkeeping loss of $200,000 and you plant stories in the press about "greedy players," "bankruptcy," and how you "can't hold out much longer." Even with a book loss of $800,000, your after-tax position would be $60,000 better than that of a non-owner.

After seven years or so, the tax benefits from depreciation of player contracts run out and most owners sell. Tax laws have placed the lifelong owner like Calvin Griffith of the Twins on the endangered species list. When a team comes to the end of its usefulness as a tax shelter for one set of owners, it is sold to another. That corporation then sets a new value on the franchise's player contracts, thus beginning another game of "depreciation."

Selling the Franchise

After two-to-seven years of tax-free prosperity the good thing begins to fade. But there is still a pot of gold at the end of the rainbow. Without exception, the owners make a profit when the franchise is sold.

The value of a major league franchise increased an average of approximately $8.5 million in the 1970s. Consider the sales history of the Philadelphia Eagles:

1933:	$2,500
1949:	$250,000
1963:	5,505,000
1967:	$14,500,000
1969:	$16,155,000
1980:	$30,000,000 (estimated value)

That's about as good an example as you can find of having your cake and eating it too.

Expansion

Expansion has become a question of *when* rather than *if*. An expansion team must buy all new player contracts, and there's really some depreciation to be had there. The established teams make out like bandits. They get big bucks for the sale of player contracts to the new clubs. (The players who are sold are usually of little value to the original team.) They get a good turnout at home for the sure victories most expansion clubs represent. They receive multi-million dollar fees from the new teams in return for the privilege of joining the rest of the league at the table set for them by the taxpayer. If the new team goes under, who cares? Its owners just do what con men down through the ages have done: change the name and move on to the next town.

Owners' Salaries

Whether or not they actually do any work, most owners carry themselves on the team payroll. For example, Dallas Mavericks' owner Norm Sonju pays himself $120,000 a year. While this is technically a business expense, in reality it is pure profit.

Remember the Minors?

Until recently, baseball players were developed in the minor leagues. In 1949 there were 59 minor leagues with 448 teams; almost everyone in the United States was within driving distance of one. By 1979 there were only 18 leagues with 158 teams.

According to Jim Bouton, "A minor league team used to be a very diverse group. There were kids right off the farm, high school dropouts, ghetto dudes, a few older guys just out of the service, and one or two college boys who always got nick-named 'Professor' or 'Harvard.' Now it's *all* college guys except for a few imported Latins. Scouts won't sign anybody else. The minor leagues are being phased out for a simple reason. It's cheaper to let colleges develop players. And college kids with more experience are easier to evaluate and less of a gamble to sign. Plus, a college draft cuts down on bidding for players. Baseball owners learned these things from NFL and NBA owners. In colleges, the instruction is better, too. They have coaches running around with stopwatches and videotape machines . . ."[3]

The owners do not contribute one penny to the educational system that provides them with their raw material.

The House That Who Built?

In 1964 the Buffalo Bills threatened to leave town if Civic

Stadium were not enlarged. The city quickly agreed. In 1970 Buffalo acquired a new resident, the NHL Sabres. But they came to town only after the city agreed to pay for $12 million worth of improvements to Memorial Auditorium. The Sabres were given a generous lease, half the concession income, and free use of the arena's offices. However, they did have to pay their own phone bill.

In 1971 the Bills showed their gratitude for the work done on Civic Stadium when they declared they would leave town if a brand new stadium weren't built. Just as U.S. industry keeps labor costs down with their constant reminder that they have an army of 30,000,000 permanently unemployed people waiting in the wings, professional teams keep their host cities in line by maintaining a pool of franchise-less cities they can threaten to move to. To placate the Bills, the Erie County legislature overlooked a host of serious civic problems and dutifully appropriated $23.5 million for the construction of Rich Stadium. Buffalo taxpayers still have to pay through the nose for Civic Stadium, now abandoned, in addition to an annual bill for $2.5 million for the new one.

If it's true that misery loves company, then Buffalo must be one happy town. The construction of the Silverdome in Pontiac, Michigan has provided the local citizens with an annual expense of $2 million to retire the stadium bonds while the city's budget deficit grows by $1.5 million a year. Who benefits from such charity? Certainly not the people of Pontiac, already devastated by the overproduction of cars. Partly because of the Silverdome debt, Pontiac schools have had to cut out much of their athletic program and lay off teachers. At the end of the 1980 school year, the school system faced an $8 million deficit. Of course, for every loser there is a winner and in this case it is William Clay Ford of the Ford Motor Company. He is the owner of the Silverdome's chief tenant, the Detroit Lions. To insure an adequate return for Mr. Ford's investment, the state of Michigan throws in an annual $800,000 subsidy.

The Superdome in New Orleans will eventually cost Louisiana taxpayers more than $135 million in interest charges alone, and most of them can't even afford to get inside.

It should be no surprise that the biggest ripoff to date has been in New York City, the nation's number one sports market. In 1972 the Yankees threatened to move to New Jersey unless the city spent $24 million to renovate Yankee Stadium, the "House That Ruth Built." CBS-TV, the Yankee owners at the time, refused to guarantee one cent of the expense. This was a wise move, since the renovation costs wound up to be something in the neighborhood of $100 million. The cost was also jobs, schools, and health care for New Yorkers. Forty-three public schools were closed for *lack of funds* during the $100 million Yankee Stadium facelift.

That the renovation ripoff was a high priority at City Hall could be seen by the speed with which the money for it was appropriated and spent. Two million dollars was supposed to go to upgrade the South Bronx ghetto which surrounds Yankee Stadium. However, the city dropped that money from the budget. Then it turned around and spent $300,000 on the Yankees, which included $7,000 for rugs for Steinbrenner's office. (Let them eat carpet!)

Seventy percent of all stadiums and arenas used by professional teams were built with public funds. In the past 25 years this has cost taxpayers $500 million. It will cost them another $6 billion by the end of the century. Meanwhile, the Milwaukee Brewers pay only one dollar on the first million admissions to County Stadium and the San Antonio Spurs pay the Hemisfair the princely sum of $1000 a game. The San Diego International Sports Arena purchased its land from the city for 20 cents an acre.

The Commissioner

The commissioners of all professional sports are chosen by the owners and serve at their sole discretion. They certainly aren't chosen for their knowledge of the sport. In 1965 a retired Air Force general, William Eckert, was selected as baseball commissioner. He had never been to a major league game in his life.

The fact that the commissioner is so beholden to the owners gives the latter a tremendous advantage in the constant battles with the players over money and playing conditions. And the owners are well aware of it. At a league meeting a couple of years ago, one NFL owner told the player representatives, "Damnit, don't be telling us Rozelle's not neutral. We pay him damn well to be neutral."[4] Convicted felon and Maple Leaf owner Harold Ballard described NHL President John Zeigler as "a nice little fellow. Insignificant. A paid employee."[5]

TV and Radio

Television and radio revenues have skyrocketed in recent years and continue to grow at a much faster rate than players' salaries. Each NFL team receives $5.8 million a year from the national television package, which would be enough to insure a profit *even if no one bought any tickets*. Each baseball team raked in more than $980,000 in 1979 and averaged more than that in local broadcast revenues. The TV contract the majors signed for 1980-83 doubles the amount each team will receive.

The networks aren't throwing their money away. They have increased the cost of a commercial minute for the baseball All-Star game and playoffs by $40,000 and have no trouble selling the spots. CBS made a clear profit of $1.8 million on the 1978 Super Bowl.

In 1979 the Phillies took the team-media romance one step further. As part of the price for the right to broadcast Philadelphia's games, WPHL-TV agreed to guarantee $600,000 of Pete Rose's $800,000 annual salary for three years. The increase in season ticket sales had already taken care of the other $200,000, so the Phillies made a profit off Pete Rose before he had even played a single game for them.

In return for the right to stick a finger in the sports pie, the media are supposed to spout the company line. When they don't, there's trouble:

- When Doug Brown of the *Baltimore Sun* wrote that then-owner Carroll Rosenbloom of the Colts had problems centered around his association with gamblers, he was dropped from the club's list of approved writers. This amounted to a professional death sentence since it cut Brown off from the inside information a sportswriter must have.

- When Hot Rod Hundley, broadcaster of New Orleans (now Utah) Jazz games, gave an interview in which he criticized Jazz coach Elgin Baylor, he was fined not by the radio station which employs him, but by Jazz chief Larry Hatfield. Unbelievably, the fine was paid.

- Remember the game in 1977 between Baltimore and New England where everyone in the United States except the officials saw Bert Jones fumble? It seems that the NFL did not want local TV stations to show the replay of that call and told them so in no uncertain terms. Bob Cochran, NFL coordinator of broadcasting, called four New York stations and told them they would be denied future use of videotape footage if they showed the replay. Despite the very real threat, all four stations showed it.

- After Bob Trumpy, former Cincinnati tight end, criticized Bengal management on his radio talk show in the spring of 1979, he was fired from his job as color man on Bengal telecasts.

Insurance

If Earl Campbell got hurt so badly he could never play again, would the Oilers get burned having to pay off the remaining years of his contract? Absolutely not.

All the owners carry insurance which protects them if an athlete cannot play, no matter what the reason. Many baseball clubs get paid every time a pitcher misses his turn in the rotation. Some teams get paid whenever certain players fail to meet specified season totals.

Older athletes are often encouraged not to come back from injuries so that the club can collect its insurance money and spend it on up-and-coming superstars.

Charley O.

Although Charlie Finley may be on his way out of baseball now, it is instructive to look at his career. Was he a crazy s.o.b. or what? Judge for yourself. When Parke Carroll, Finley's first general manager at Kansas City, died unexpectedly, his widow asked Finley for the $50,000 still owed on Carroll's contract. He refused to give it to her. She sued but still never got the money.

But Charlie Finley was not crazy. Despite low attendance, the Oakland A's made an annual profit of between $600,000 and $1,300,000, not including tax benefits. Under Finley, the A's had the lowest player payroll in baseball, spent absolutely no money on promotion, and had no full-time scouts or minor league pitching or hitting instructors. Finley's contract with the Oakland Coliseum gave him one-fourth of all parking and concession revenues, and he paid only $125,000 in rent per season. After the A's won their World Championships, he sold every player he could for cash. That was his plan from the very beginning.

Once Finley's depreciation benefits ran dry, he sold the team to the Haas family for $8 million more than he paid for it. They will pay for it with the fortune they've made from their non-union Levi Strauss plants.

Finley was the first baseball man to take ownership to its logical conclusion. He probably realized that if every owner acted the same way it would destroy the game. But as long as there was room for one, Charley was the man.

The real position of all the owners, from Charlie Finley to Gulf and Western Corporation, can be summed up by the fact that at the beginning of baseball's player-management negotiations for the past twelve years, a representative of the owners has stated, "The clubs have not, do not, and will not make any claim of financial difficulty."

The Athletes: Without a Hot Bat, It's a Cold World

**And it's just like a Calcutta auction
Where the players get bought and sold
Ladies and gentlemen, lay your money down
Please don't believe all that you get told***

There is no question that the modern professional athlete is somewhat better off than his counterparts of yesteryear. The salaries are higher. There is a limited degree of control by the players over where they will work. And a select few have achieved financial security with their health intact.

"Well, now they've taken the kneecap out of my left knee, my ankles were broken and fixed, but I can't straighten either of my arms anymore."[1]

GEORGE MIKAN, basketball's
"Player of the Half-Century"

Today it is unheard of for any star to get the DiMaggio treatment. In 1942 the Yankee Clipper was offered a $5,000 pay cut after he had hit safely in 56 straight games the year before.

Times are changing. The bidding wars between rival leagues are ancient history. That giant of the past thirty years, the United States economy, fueled the tremendous expansion of professional sports. Now its bold stride has become a directionless limp. When the international economic order comes crashing down in a shower of credit cards in the 1980s, the gravy days for a handful of professional athletes will be over.

It is· high time to lay to rest all the notions about the pampered, overpaid athlete who pushes the owners around. Let the funeral begin.

You Can't Tell the Salaries
Without a Contract

How much money do professional athletes really make? Admit it, you think you know. Well, how did you find out? If you have seen the actual player contract, you know. But if you just read about it in the papers, (DR. J. INKS NEW FIVE MILLION DOLLAR PACT!), you don't. The guy who wrote the story hasn't seen the contract either. He just made up the figures or got them from the owner, which amounts to the same thing.

When it was gospel that Warren Spahn made $110,000 a year, it was truth that he got $70,000. When John Matuszak was the number one draft pick of the Houston Oilers, the press let everyone know that he had signed a four-year, $300,000 contract. A year later the truth came out in court: a $30,000 bonus and $25,000 a year. That's less than a roller in a steel mill makes. Joe Namath's celebrated rookie contract actually provided only a $25,000 base salary, with the rest of the money spread out over decades and conditional upon the survival of the franchise.

Nowadays there is another cog in the machinery of salary escalation besides the owners and the presses at the U.S. mint: the agent. Many agents inflate the value of the contracts they negotiate in order to advertise their abilities to other athletes. Even Pat Williams, right-hand man for 76er owner Fitz Dixon, says, "I'd like to retire on the difference between the actual numbers and what's reported."[2]

Consider a man we all think has it made: a first-round pick in the NBA draft. Our man John Doe is a 6-7, 210 lb. swingman who just led his school to the NCAA championship. Shooting, rebounding, defense, ballhandling—he can do it all. But John has a problem. Academically, he's only halfway through his junior year. He's not stupid, but he's unprepared for the owners and their slick lawyers. So he turns to an agent. In reality, the agents have already turned on him. They have been stuffing money in his pockets since high school with the goal of getting his signature on a personal services contract. Larry Collins of Texas A&I and the Browns once had four agents at the same time. John is lucky and winds up with a relatively honest agent, at least a better one than Richard Sorkin. Sorkin was charged with stealing money from more than a dozen of his clients.

The agent gets ten percent of John's total compensation package right off the top, although John won't get all of his share for at least ten years. The agent also gets 25 percent of all endorsement income. John chooses to take most of what's left in various forms of deferred income. Something for a rainy day. A wise move by the youngster, right? Maybe. In effect, he is giving the owner an interest-free loan. A $100,000 cash annuity costs the team only $21 a week. When it comes time to collect the money in ten or twenty years, John Doe will be paid in inflated dollars worth less than half what they were worth when he signed.

Ominously, most deferred payments are guaranteed by the franchise and not by the owners or their heirs. If the team has gone under before you go to collect those long-awaited goodies...you don't get a dime. And believe me, in twenty years most of today's teams will be out of business.

Maybe salaries haven't risen all that much. In 1932 Babe Ruth made $80,000 a year which is equivalent to $590,000 in 1980.

To figure out what a pro athlete really makes, you have to figure in the years of preparation. Take the case of Dr. J. When he was coming up on Long Island, he used to work all day and through the evening at a local playground. Besides playing ball, he did hours of jumping drills every day. When the park closed at 11 PM the Doctor would stay and work on his jump shot for hours. As he says himself, "If a player practices as long as I did, he could go to his left, go to his right as well as I do."[3] Work, work, and more work. Professional athletes have paid the price and deserve everything they get. When you figure in the thousands and thousands of hours of practice and conditioning, a star athlete makes about what a plumber does. A fringe player hovers in the vicinity of minimum wage.

"I've watched Julius Erving many times and he's poetry in motion. To watch him and see what he can do with his body— it's fantastic. But people don't see the years spent in working up to that point."[4]

>   *MAX ZASLOFSKY, NBA All-Star*
>   *once drafted ahead of Cousy*

"There isn't a check big enough to pay me back."[5]
>   *EARL CAMPBELL*

Set For Life?

The professional athlete has very little security. The baseball pension plan is the strongest in sports. Yet, as of April, 1978, only 611 players had received payment from it. In every professional sport the average athlete does not play long enough to qualify for a pension. Picture this: You've had three knee operations and your chosen career is over well before you're thirty. You can't walk without pain and a full night's sleep is a fading memory. If you are black or Latin, there is almost no chance you will get a coaching or front office job. Twenty-five years from now you may get a pension—if the fund is still solvent. It's really the same as in private industry. For example, General Motors has a future pension liability of over $6 billion that it has no funds set aside to cover. Ditto for U.S. Steel to the tune of $1 billion. Will there be any money for you or me or Rob Lytle or Amos Otis when we retire?

Long-term contracts are on the way out. Only 70 of the 1,476 players in the NFL have no-cut contracts. What fans don't understand is that most three- or four-year contracts are in reality three or four consecutive one-year contracts. At the end of each year the owner has the option to get rid of the athlete for any reason whatsoever. For example, in the spring of 1979 the Mets gave Lenny Randle his unconditional release. Although Randle had three years left to go on a contract allegedly worth $500,000, all he got was a plane ticket home.

"There were times when you had five year guarantees; well, I don't believe you will see that much anymore; that's on the way out."[6]

LENNY WILKINS

Countless athletes, from Dick Butkus to jockey Ron Turcotte, have had their careers ended by injuries and/or surgery. Many must live with severe pain all their lives, and they find that jobs are hard to get. Very few get any kind of disability. All the owners want to know is "What have you done for me lately?"

This brings us to the team doctors. The key word here is team, not doctor. There may be many fine and ethical team physicians but the setup is bogus from the start. In the first place, team doctors are employed by the club when they should be under contract to their patients, the players. Dr. Arthur Pappas of the Red Sox even owns 4 percent of the team. In 67 grievances handled by the NFL Players Association, the team doctors testified for the owners in every single case.

I don't know if anyone can prove that a team doctor ever intentionally made an incorrect diagnosis just to get an athlete back into a game, but there does seem to be a pattern. Willie Randolph of the Yankees was told that his knee was only bruised when, in fact, he had a torn cartilage that required surgery. Bill Walton, Herb Lusk of the Philadelphia Eagles, and Jimmy DuBose of Tampa Bay all played entire seasons with broken bones that had been diagnosed as "minor injuries." Mike Robitaille, a defenseman for the Vancouver Canucks in the NHL, suffered a severe spinal cord contusion during a game and had to be dragged from the ice. The team doctor prescribed a shot of Courvoisier and a good night's sleep. When Robitaille insisted on going to the hospital the next day, management labelled him a "con artist" and a "chronic complainer." Today Mike Robitaille suffers from a permanent spinal cord injury which causes his arms and legs to jerk involuntarily and has impaired his sex life. Bobby Gross of the Portland Trailblazers saw his ankle shatter after it was injected with Marcaine and he was sent back into a game...

"I've been instructed by the Yankees, 'Don't tell the player what's wrong with him.'"[7]
        DR. MAURICE COWEN, former Yankee team doctor

Dr. Jay Malkoff quit as team physician for the San Diego Sockers soccer team after the coach insisted that he allow a player with a fractured cheekbone to return to the game.

"The day I was operated on John Ralston wanted a walkie-talkie hooked up from my operating table to his office. Then as soon as they cut me open, they could radio back that he could go ahead and get another tackle. That's the kind of coldness I had seen happen to hundreds of guys before, but all of a sudden, it was upon me."[8]
        MIKE CURRENT, NFL lineman

Standing on Shaky Ground

The number of jobs in professional sports continues to decline. NBA rosters have been cut from 12 to 11 and baseball teams now carry 24 players most of the time instead of the traditional 25. If a guy refuses to play when hurt or if his game slips a little, there are always plenty of hungry players waiting to take his place. When the Detroit Pistons needed a quick mid-season replacement at guard in 1979, they plucked Dennis Boyd from his job as a security guard at a Chrysler plant.

Having quit their day jobs, what happens to the Dennis Boyds of this world if they don't become career pros?

> **Boy you should be grateful**
> **To get your foot inside the door**
> **You know there's thousands out there**
> **Who would take your place**
> **This attitude of yours, my son**
> **Well it lacks the due respect**

You bite the hand that feeds you
Even if you're never fed*

I'll give you 10-1 that tomorrow's sports page, wherever you live, will carry a story about athletes' greed. But it won't carry stories like the following:

- Charlie Criss used two weeks of vacation from his job to go to a Knicks training camp. He survived the first few cuts, overstayed his vacation by one day, and lost his job. The next week the Knicks cut him.

- Players are pressured into playing winter ball in Latin America, where they get sick from the food and insect bites.

- Thirty-two players paid their way to Cincinnati in 1979 so they could display their wares for NBA coaches at Ron Grinker's annual flesh market at Riverfront Coliseum. Some barely had enough to eat during the tryouts, and Pop Green from Baton Rouge didn't even have a way to get back home.

- Athletes such as Craig Morton, Joe Louis, Lance Alworth, Bobby Nystrom, Johnny Neumann, and Eddie Arcaro have been swindled into bankruptcy.

"You can't imagine what all that moving and uncertainty does to a family. Planning to be in one place for the season, then ending up someplace else. Uprooting the kids, uprooting Katie. New apartments, new friends. Our mail always lost in some deadletter office."[9]

JOHN STOFA, quarterback for five pro teams

They Doth Protest Too Much

Little-noticed behind the headlines, some forms of compensation are falling. Remember the baseball bonus baby? If you do, you're older than you think. He is almost non-existent today because the colleges, at our expense, have replaced the

---

*From "Midwest Midnight" by M. Gee and Michael Stanley. © Michael Stanley Music (ASCAP). All rights reserved.

minors. Top draft choices seldom get no-cut contracts anymore. The first player taken in the 1977 NBA draft, Kent Benson, received about $500,000 less than his counterpart for 1972, Marvin Barnes. Twenty-five years ago, 35 percent of the game's revenues went to baseball players' salaries. Today their share is only 26 percent. The slice of the pie for NFL players has fallen from 45 to 25 percent.

But forget all this. Do the owners make money off the modern superstar or not? What's the bottom line? A study by the Brookings Institute showed that in a metropolitan area of two million people a star basketball player who makes the difference between winning and losing ten games a year will generate an extra 2,340 fans per game. That's approximately $800,000 a year in additional income for the team's owners. This is more than any basketball player makes. Vince Gennaro, president of Sport Planning Associates, calculated the value of Jim Rice to the Boston Red Sox as $1,098,526 a year. Warner Communications, which owns the New York Cosmos, made a clear profit of $2 million from Pele. When Houston signed Earl Campbell, they immediately sold an additional 5,036 season tickets for a total of $700,000. That accounted for at least half the cost of Campbell's contract before he ever touched the ball. Rod Carew's signature on the dotted line meant an additional 4,543 season tickets worth $1.6 million for the California Angels.

When you add in the money from parking and concessions that the players bring in by attracting fans (an average of 80 cents net per fan), the muddy waters begin to clear.

If the owners are on the verge of bankruptcy, they need new accountants.

Tumbling Dice

Tens of millions of people bet on sports and nobody seems too uptight about it. Still, the money from gambling goes to fund drugs, prostitution, and labor racketeering, so somebody has to get the blame for it. Human nature? It's in the bones of mankind to gamble and that's the way it'll always be. Well, maybe. But human nature is too vague to be a varsity scapegoat. We need some names!

Connie Hawkins? He once accepted a $50 loan from some-one he didn't know who was later convicted of fixing basket-ball games. As a result, Hawkins was barred from both col-lege ball and the NBA. The fact that he never did shave points and suffered from malnutrition at the time of the loan doesn't matter. Maybe he's to blame for all the problems gambling brings with it.

Or maybe the villain is Roger Brown. Once called the Elgin Baylor of the ABA, Brown was alleged to have been involved in a point-shaving scheme at the University of Dayton. As a result he was banned for life from the NBA. Could it be that Roger Brown, acquitted in the Dayton scandal and now scuf-fling in semi-pro ball, is responsible?

Maybe it's the fault of the 1919 Black Sox. They started the whole thing when they threw a couple of World Series games because they literally could not live on the salaries the owners were paying.

Why is it always the players (Alex Karras, Paul Hornung, Joe Namath, Denny McLain) who get in hot water?

When questions were raised about his bar, Bachelor's III, Joe Namath hired a private detective to see if gambling figures were using it to approach players. No. A check was made with the New York Police Department. Clean. Pete Rozelle sup-posedly had dates, times, and places. But he refused to show this evidence to Namath or anyone else. He has never released any proof of his accusations. But by dragging Joe Namath's name through the mud he has cast a shadow that will remain forever.

And when he discovered that Oakland Raider owner Al Davis was part-owner of a shopping center connected with Nevada gambling interests, Pete Rozelle did nothing.

I defy any owner to testify under oath that he does not bet on games.

Wake Up! It's Time to Catch the Plane and Get Some Sleep!

Some astute observers have noticed that professional athletes occasionally seem to put out less than a 100 percent effort. Well, they may be right but it's not because the athletes are lazy. They're *tired*.

> *"Only eighteen more."*[10]—*Dave DeBusschere*
> *"Not yet. It's too early to start counting."*[10]—*Bill Bradley*

The increased length of the schedule is nothing more than a sports version of industrial speed-up and overtime. It has exactly the same effects: more injuries, less output, lower quality. And man, do you ever get tired! When *you* have to work ten, twelve, or sixteen hours a day, don't you coast whenever you can? Especially if you're forced to work when you're hurt? It's no different for professional athletes. It just seems that way because people pay to watch them work.

I doubt that many fans would feel like busting their butts if they were bounced around the country like professional athletes are. For example, in 1979 the Bulls played a game in Chicago, flew to Baltimore for another game, flew back to Chicago for another game, and then on to New York for yet another game. All in less than 96 hours.

Professional teams rarely fly charters. That leaves plenty of time to sit around on buses, sit around in airports, and fall asleep in coffee shops. "Hey mister, how's the weather up there?" "Are you guys really the Phillies?"

Only eighteen more...

Once upon a time you knew what time of year it was by the sport displayed on the silver screen at the corner bar. But the owners' need for more and more games has created winter baseball and summer basketball.

If you thought it was cold during the 1979 World Series, wait until there are three divisions in each league. The extra set of playoffs could extend the baseball season until Halloween. (Bowie Kuhn will have to put his coat on.) Pitching in the cold has ruined many a player's arm. Lee Cain of the Tigers receives workmen's compensation for it. The mind boggles at the thought of a World Series between Montreal and Toronto.

No description of playing conditions would be complete without a word on artificial turf. It causes more injuries and doesn't even save money. When the San Francisco Board of Supervisors considered the installation of artificial turf at

Candlestick Park, they discovered it would cost $40,000 more than natural grass.

Why, owners, why?

Players' Unions

The past decade has seen the various players' associations become a significant force in the sports world. On the surface, these unions seem powerful, and indeed they have forced many concessions from the owners. But all this happened during a time when the economy was still expanding and the owners' businesses, inside and outside of sports, were prospering. But as the economic worm turns, the sports robin must follow.

This was evident during the 1980 baseball negotiations. The corporations that own most major league teams are beset by many problems including a falling rate of profit, a decline in the growth of productivity, and the loss of many foreign markets. In this situation, the stockholders of these corporations were no longer in a position to allow their errand boys to make further concessions to the players and they didn't. They chose as chief negotiater a Mr. Ray Grebey, one-time Inland Steel coke plant foreman and a labor relations honcho at General Electric for 21 years. While the final agreement didn't change things that much, the owners secured the first steps toward the destruction of free agency. Not that they were really worried about a player strike on Memorial Day or any other day. While a long strike or lockout would financially ruin most professional athletes and rip the unions to shreds, for the owners it would be just another tax break.

If the players are to avoid crushing defeats in the future, they must remedy the internal weaknesses they share with the rest of organized labor. They must move beyond lip service in dealing with the discrimination that permeates professional sports. They must enforce a closed shop and not allow their leaders to be picked off.

On some fronts, the athletes have already begun to fight back. Recently six players associations banded together to form the Professional Atheletes International (PAI). It now has over 3,000 members and may affiliate with the AFL-CIO.

Baseball players are building a defense fund and have secured the right to get all agreements translated into Spanish at the owners' expense.

These steps are significant but woefully insufficient. They do not end the isolation and vulnerability of the athletes. Just as the AFL-CIO has failed to educate the public about the real causes of inflation and unemployment, the players' unions have allowed the corporate puppets in the media free reign to spread their lies about professional sports. The natural ally of the athlete is the fan who sits outside the corporate box, but nothing short of a nationwide educational campaign can make that alliance a reality.

The Fans:
No Unemployed
Need Apply

"CONGRESS BANS ALL WORKING PEOPLE FROM NFL GAMES!" Science fiction? If you want to go to a Cowboy game at Texas Stadium, you first have to buy a season ticket for $150. But to be allowed to buy a season ticket you have to purchase a stadium bond at a minimum cost of $250. Somehow you scrape together the money and buy that season ticket after four years on a waiting list. You drive to the stadium in eager anticipation of the first game. You settle into your seat, but it's a hot September day and you're thirsty. You scan the stadium for a beer vendor but you can't see one anywhere. There's still twenty minutes until the kickoff so you truck on down to the concession stand. But they don't sell beer. A passing Exxon executive informs you that the only way to get a beer in Texas Stadium is to buy a membership at the Stadium Club. You decide you're not *that* thirsty.

"Yes, I'd say we lost a whole group in the twelve-to-twenty thousand-dollar-a-year salary range who couldn't afford to buy bonds. If we discriminated against them, we discriminated against them. But no more than all America discriminates against people who don't have enough money to buy everything they want."[1]

CLINT MURCHISON, Cowboy owner

The Broncos, the Redskins (who play in RFK Stadium, officially a national park built with our tax money), and the

Giants sell only season tickets. But even if you can find a single game ticket, you still may not be able to afford it. The Red Sox raised their ticket prices in 1979 after they had made a $3 million profit with the smallest park in baseball. The Atlanta Braves have eliminated all children's tickets. In the NBA almost all good seats are sold as season tickets. Unless you own a pair of binoculars, you'll be doing business with the scalpers. How do they get ahold of single-game season ticket seats, anyway?

The Price Is Wrong

What drives ticket prices through the roof? It is not player salaries. Increases in wages don't cause price increases, as we all learned during the Nixon wage freeze. Any half-decent economist will tell you that when you print money that is not backed up by gold, each dollar is worth less. This means it takes more dollars to buy a third base seat and that, ladies and gentlemen, is inflation.

According to Bill Melchioni of the New Jersey Nets front office, ticket prices are tied to only two things: "how successful your team is and what the market is willing to pay."[2] The Toronto Blue Jays are a perennial last-place team but they have the eighth-highest ticket prices in baseball.

In the past forty years, salaries have gone up and down but ticket prices have never been reduced. Leigh Steinberg, an agent from Los Angeles, represents more than thirty athletes. In every contract he has negotiated, he has attempted to include a clause whereby the athlete would take a pay cut every time the owner lowered prices. In every case, the owners refused to sign.

So who does buy all the tickets? Some rich individuals certainly do. But most of the tickets go to corporations. In 1977 corporations purchased 78 percent of all baseball season tickets, accounted for 34 percent of all baseball attendance, and were responsible for 42 percent of baseball's revenue. Nearly half the teams in the National Hockey League sell out the entire year on a season-ticket basis. Corporate purchases account for 54 percent of the total.

You may not know a jump shot from an audible but you

still pay for tickets. Not for yourself, not for your nephew, but for General Motors and Bethlehem Steel. When these corporations build stadium boxes or buy season tickets, they just write it off their taxes as a business expense. Less taxes for them means more for you.

TV or Not TV

The media loves to chastise the modern athlete for lack of loyalty and devotion to the game. On April 9, 1978, John Havlicek played his last game. The game was on national television and Hondo scored nine points in the last 55 seconds but nobody saw it. With two minutes left in the game, CBS cut away to a Cadillac commercial and then to the Masters' golf tournament. With tears in his loyal eyes, Barry Frank of CBS summed it up: "It was not a tough call to make. I'd do it again even if Havlicek scored twenty points in the last two minutes."[3]

The plain truth is that the networks are not concerned just with ratings. Several years ago *LOOK* magazine informed tens of thousands of people that they would no longer be *allowed* to subscribe because they did not make enough money to interest advertisers. Television is basically the same. Golf does not get good ratings, but it attracts a wealthy audience and the sponsors who sell luxury items wait in line to get at it. Bud buys baseball; Cadillac buys golf.

A sport like basketball, although infinitely more popular than golf, gets relatively less exposure because so many hoop fans just don't make enough money to interest the "better" sponsors. Every tennis tournament in the world seems to wind up on the tube while many important basketball games never grace the silver screen. It's really another form of discrimination. Basketball is often called the national sport of black people. Black family income averages nearly $6,000 a year less than that of white families. That's $6,000 less to put in the pockets of television sponsors. Don't you think millions of people would like to watch the finals of a tournament like the Rucker in Harlem? "Yeah," CBS would say. "Millions of poor people."

As pay TV comes to dominate sports broadcasting, the problem will get worse. More and more people will be cut off from sports altogether. Perhaps they'll finally lift the blackouts of the games we won't be able to afford to watch on TV anyway.

The Olympics:
If the Shoe Fits,
Sell It!

Dateline: Moscow. It was the best of Olympics, it was the worst of Olympics.

It was one of the best because the level of performance was so high. Even with powerhouses like the United States and West Germany on the sidelines, thirty-five world records were set— only one fewer than at Montreal in 1976. Sixty-two Olympic records were set—only six fewer than the previous Games.

It was the worst of Olympics only because the media in the United States kept telling us so. Actually, I don't know myself. Although for four years I had looked forward to watching the 1980 Olympics, they weren't on. I pay $22 a month for cablevision and they have around-the-clock sports channels but the Olympics weren't on. The Coe-Ovett duels, incredible new records in the high jump, pole vault, and hammer throw; the end of Alexeyev's career; a new basketball champion; eight new world records in swimming; Stevenson, the first heavyweight to win three golds. Sounds like a pretty good Olympics to me.

Certainly it would have been better without the boycott, if all the athletes who wanted to go, who deserved to go, had been allowed to compete. But that was not to be. Yet even though the Moscow Games squeezed through, the Olympics are in big trouble and everybody knows it. How did we get in this mess—the financial boondoggles at Montreal and Lake Placid, the attempted sabotage of the 1980 Games, the impending catastrophe at Los Angeles in 1984?

To understand where the Olympics are going, we need to take a look at where they've been. Brief. Oversimplified. But true.

Ancient Greece

Politics and sports are not an alien mixture like oil and water. They're more like men and women, and have been together nearly as long.

Today we hear a lot of crying about how the Olympics have strayed from the "noble and lofty ideals" of the ancient Greek games. This was pure sport where young men of vision and grace competed solely to test their skills. Money was of no importance to these bold lads.

Oh yeah? In fact, the ancient Olympics were even more screwed up than the current ones. Women were not allowed to compete or even to watch, under penalty of death. Under these circumtances they were forced to organize their own secret competitions. Slaves made up a big part of the population of ancient Greece but they too were banned from the Olympics. Personally, that is just what I would expect from a society based on the labor of slaves. But I'm not the one who extols the virtues of ancient Greece. In fact, it was only kings and chieftans and the warriors who protected them who were allowed to compete.

Amateurism didn't begin in Greece; professionalism did. The first six Olympiads had an up-front schedule of cash prizes. After that, the payoffs merely shifted from over the pedestal to under the table.

The ancient Greeks cheated too:

- In the 98th Olympics, Eupous of Thesaly bribed his opponents in boxing.
- In the 112th Olympics, Callippus of Athens bribed his opponents in the pentathlon.
- In the 178th Olympics, a wrestler from Rhodes bribed his opponents.
- In the 192nd Olympics, Damonicus bribed the father of Sosander to enable his son to win the wrestling final.

Why go to all that trouble? Because an Olympic champion stood to collect as much as 500 drachmas, which put him in the same tax bracket as Mark Spitz or Bruce Jenner today.

The Origins of the Modern Olympics

Hundreds of millions of people enjoy the Olympics so perhaps we do owe a debt of gratitude to Baron Pierre de Coubertin, the man who played a key role in resurrecting the Olympics in Athens in 1896. But the myth that de Coubertin was only interested in "pure, ideal" sport (sound familiar?) has got to go because it just isn't true. The real impetus behind his efforts was the political situation in France, his homeland. In 1871, the French had been beaten to a pulp in the Franco-Prussian War. The leaders of France's Third Republic decided that it was in the interest of French *military objectives* in Europe to initiate a program of mass physical education. The idea of organized recreation for the masses was very new and de Coubertin met great resistance when he insisted that emphasis in any Olympics be on the participation of the many rather than the excellence of the few. To help facilitate the military preparedness of French youth, the French Sports Union was formed in 1887; in 1891 de Coubertin became its General Secretary.

Those who still try to hang the albatross of amateurism around our necks and justify it as a tradition might do well to chew on the following words of de Coubertin: "The actual rules are wicked... It is the sportsman's spirit that interests me and not respect of that ridiculous English concept that allows only millionaires to dedicate themselves to sports..."

Given the military motives for the initial organization of mass sports and the subsequent revival of the Olympic Games, it should be no surprise that nationalism in international sport continues to plague us. The current world economic crisis only makes it worse. We are asked to believe that everything will be all right if our hockey team beats the Soviets. This merely continues a tradition that was begun in the United States. Following smashing U.S. triumphs at the 1900 Olympics, the American press invented the concept of the Olympics as a contest between nations rather than individuals. And in 1906 *The New York Times* devised a scoring system to determine which nation had "won" the Olympics. The 1920 Olympics had originally been awarded to

Hungary but, perhaps due to the abortive post-war revolution by Hungarian workers, it was transferred to Antwerp. Yet the International Olympic Committee (IOC) saw no problem in awarding the 1936 Games to Nazi Germany.

1936: The Hitler Olympics

The announcement that the 1936 Summer Games would be held in Berlin resulted in a firestorm of world protest. In the United States a movement to boycott the Olympics was supported by a wide cross-section of the population: twenty Olympic champions, religious organizations, the American Federation of Labor, the NAACP, and the AAU. Without the sanction of the AAU, no athlete could compete in Berlin. In November 1933 the AAU declared that no athlete would be allowed to compete unless there was an immediate reversal of Nazi policies. In August 1935, the largest sports protest in U.S. history took place. Twenty thousand people filled Madison Square Garden in support of the boycott.

Yet Avery Brundage, chairman of the U.S. Olympic Committee (USOC) and an avowed admirer of Hitler, worked night and day to suppress the boycott. *After* he had ordered U.S. athletes to prepare for the Games, Brundage travelled to Berlin to investigate charges of persecution of Jews. Despite the general exclusion of Jews from German life (including sports—many world-class Jewish athletes had already been forced to flee), despite the book burnings and the dismemberment of the trade unions, Brundage returned to sing the praises of the Third Reich. It was fitting that the final vote of the USOC to accept the Olympic invitation took place at the New York Athletic Club, which barred Jews and blacks from membership.

Jews were also banned from the 1936 Winter Olympics held in Germisch, Germany. Although this was hardly "an immediate reversal of Nazi policies," the AAU eventually did sanction U.S. athletes to go to Berlin. As General Charles Sherrill, member of both the USOC and IOC, put it at the time, "It does not concern me one bit the way the Jews are being treated in Germany any more than the lynchings in the South of our own country."[1]

Hitler had confidently predicted that Germany's "Aryan supermen" would sweep the Olympics and so the victories of Jesse Owens and other blacks caused a lot of problems in Berlin. All sorts of "theories" were trotted out to explain away the ability of the black athletes. One English newspaper went so far as to claim that they acquired their speed through special leg operations.

After the Games concluded, the Berlin Olympic Village became the home of the German army that would soon invade Poland. Back in New York Avery Brundage appeared before a mass rally of the German-American Bund and declared, "No nation since ancient Greece has displayed a more truly national public interest in the Olympic spirit than you find in Germany. We can learn much from Germany..."[2]

1968: The Black Boycott

The significance of the 1968 Games in Mexico City partly lies in the incredible onslaught on the outer limits of human performance that took place there. Record after record was broken, with the coup de grace an unbelievable 29 '2½ " broad jump by Bob Beamon. These Olympics also witnessed the very rare political intersection of Africa, the Caribbean, the United States, and Latin America.

On November 23, 1967, an historic resolution was unanimously passed at the Black Youth Conference in Los Angeles. It cited the hypocrisy of the U.S. government's claim to wear the mantle of leader of the "free world" while it cooperated in maintaining poverty for blacks. It further stated that U.S. black athletes would not compete in the Olympics or in any meet where athletes from Rhodesia (now Zimbabwe) or South Africa participated.

The reaction of the media and sports establishment was hysteria. They just couldn't believe the *ingratitude* of it all. The *New York Daily News* called the vote on the resolution "Mob Rule In Los Angeles." Otis Burrell, a conference participant and world-class athlete, was notified that he was no longer welcome at the Christmas job he had worked for three years. Death threats became common.

The boycott movement grew to become the Olympic Project for Human Rights (OPHR) and its leaders included Harry Edwards, Louis Lomax, and Martin Luther King, Jr. The main purpose of the OPHR was exposure of the second-class status of blacks, and particularly black athletes, in the United States. The OPHR pointed out over and over again that the limited success of a few black athletes had done nothing to solve problems such as 50 percent unemployment for black youth.

Sprinter Tommie Smith declared his willingness to give up not only the Olympics but his life itself for any effort that might help bring about equality. Sportswriter Jim Murray of *The Los Angeles Times* compared Tommie to "a child who holds his breath to make his parents feel bad."[3] While Jim Murray was having a high old time on his expense account, Tommie Smith was growing up sharing a bed with three other children. His parents were California farmworkers who picked cotton for 90 cents an hour.

At the same time that 1968 All-Americans Kareem Abdul-Jabbar, Lucius Allen, Mike Warren, and Bill Hewitt refused to try out for the Olympic basketball team, the Caribbean nations of Guyana, Trinidad, and Barbados were joining another kind of boycott. This one was designed to keep South Africa out of the Olympics as a protest against apartheid.

The movement to isolate South Africa athletically had ebbed and flowed throughout the 1960s. Although the South Africans had been barred from the Tokyo Games in 1964, the IOC reversed its decision in 1968 and welcomed them back into the fold. This action spread the anti-apartheid movement across the globe. South Africa had staunch supporters such as the United States and New Zealand. But each passing day brought another country's announcement that it would not compete in the Olympics with South Africa.

Faced with the gradual disintegration of the Olympic movement and the financially disastrous possibility that the socialist countries might join the boycott, the IOC gave in. Reluctantly, they barred South Africa from the Olympics. (Shell Oil helped to ease the pain when it gave South Africa the money to hold its own segregated sports festival the following year.)

Meanwhile, back in Mexico City the hundreds of millions of dollars spent on the Olympic Games in such a poor country had increased social tensions almost to the breaking point. Throughout the summer there had been huge demonstrations demanding that money be spent on food and shelter instead of on the Olympics.

As the athletes gathered at the Olympic Village in early fall, plans for more demonstrations were made. In anticipation, the army occupied schools and colleges throughout Mexico City. On a Wednesday evening students held a rally at the Plaza de las Tres Culturas. Thousands readied for a march on a nearby school. But a leader of the city-wide student strike announced that the march had been called off—too many soliders, too many guns. Suddenly a green flare arched over the plaza and the courtyard exploded in gunfire. For nearly three hours, soldiers emptied their weapons into the courtyard. Thirty-four dead, hundreds wounded.

The Olympics must go on!

And go on they did. By now the tactics of the OPHR had changed. Unable to get sufficient unity to pull off a solid boycott, it was decided that each athlete would demonstrate his or her solidarity with the struggles of American blacks in an individual way. Tommie Smith won the gold medal in the 200-meter dash and John Carlos won the bronze. They mounted the victory stand shoeless, each wearing a black glove. They were joined by silver medalist Peter Norman of Australia, who wore the official badge of the OPHR. As the national anthem was played, Smith and Carlos raised their gloved fists and bowed their heads. They were immediately thrown off the team and given only 48 hours to leave the Olympic Village.

Three days later, three other American blacks—Lee Evans, Larry James, Ron Freeman—swept the 400-meter dash. At the victory celebration, all three wore black berets and raised their fists as their names were called. Yet they were not sent home because they were all on the team for the upcoming 1600-meter relay. Smith and Carlos had no more races left.

1980: A New Kind of Boycott

1980 saw a new kind of boycott movement forced upon the world by President Jimmy Carter. His motives were obvious:

to use the crudest "patriotic" appeals to take our minds off the impending depression; to allow the government to push through yet another increase in the military budget at the expense of jobs and education.

In many ways this was a new kind of boycott. Countries which had always opposed past boycotts were eager to get in on this one. Dictatorships like Chile, Taiwan and Saudi Arabia couldn't wait to tell the world they wouldn't go.

This boycott had almost no support from athletes. Over 150 U.S. Winter Olympic athletes signed a petition against it. Half a dozen organizations sprang up around the country which were led by athletes and fought for the right to go to Moscow. Over 90 percent of Canada's athletes sent telegrams to their prime minister opposing the boycott. When President Carter held a reception on the White House lawn for the U.S. "Olympic team" during the Summer Olympics, many athletes refused to attend (including 27 out of 30 women rowers).

All previous boycott efforts had grass roots involvement and organization. This one was run from the top down. It was clear that the Carter Administration had not sought and did not want second opinions. At the inaugural meeting of the new national track organization, the Athletics Congress, a phone call was made to Carter requesting that he attend or send a representative to discuss the boycott. He refused. Speedskater Eric Heiden tried to discuss the boycott with him. Silence.

In 1936 it was clear to all what the Nazis were up to. In 1968 it was obvious that blacks were second-class citizens in both the United States and South Africa. What about Afghanistan in 1980?

Now I don't know a lot about Afghanistan. But I doubt very much that you do either. Probably not more than one American in a hundred can state a single fact about Afghanistan. When we know as much about Afghanistan as we did about Germany, the United States, or South Africa, *then* we will be in a position to make decisions.

We have merely taken the government's word for what is happening there. Let's take a look at the past record of the United States government on the truth of its public statements. We were lied to about the U-2 incident. We were lied to about the Bay of Pigs. We were lied to about the Kennedy assasination. We were lied to about the Gulf of Tonkin. We were lied to about Watergate. We were lied to about Three Mile Island. We were lied to about the Love Canal.

Only a person intent on suicide should take the word of the U.S. government at face value. I speak from experience. In the fall of 1964 I had just finished Navy boot camp and was stationed aboard the destroyer *USS John W. Thomason.* A week before we were to sail for Vietnam, I came down with food poisoning. I was terrified. Not for my health, but because I might not be able to go overseas. The President of my country had told me that there was a small freedom-loving nation with a democratic government that had been invaded by a hated enemy from the north. The people in the south wanted our help. I believed President Johnson and I wanted to go in the worst way.

After several trips to Vietnam I began to realize that President Johnson was a liar. The government of South Vietnam was a dictatorship run by a bunch of drug pushers and murderers. The people of the south only wanted us to go away. The U.S. government had forcibly prevented the peaceful reunification of the country a decade earlier. My Lai was standard operating procedure and millions of Indochinese never lived to talk about it.

A lot of my friends would have loved to watch the 1980 Olympics but the reception isn't too good in bodybags. I had nightmares for fifteen years about the people I was forced to kill, many of them women and children.

President Carter promised to cut the military budget but instead he increased it. He promised to be a friend of labor and to repeal the Taft-Hartley Act. Instead he used it against the miners. Let's make sure we get the facts from more objective sources before we get involved in any more boycotts, "rescues," or wars.

Heads I Win, Tails You Lose

The U.S. government has never missed an opportunity to take credit for the success of our international athletes. Yet it does nothing to help our athletes train or compete. And it brazenly claims that non-help is the best way, the only way.

But when the government wants athletes *not to compete*, you can't get away from it. Threats, intimidation, money for "alternate competitions"; anything goes to get athletes *not to compete*. Not one penny is available when they want *to compete*. During the 1980 Olympics, the Carter Administration gave the U.S. Olympic Committee several million dollars as the payoff for its support of the boycott. This is in the great American tradition of paying farmers not to grow food. Indeed, the big grain companies will receive hundreds of millions of dollars for witholding grain from the Soviet Union. What will our athletes get?

"Carter said 'we' are going to boycott the Olympics. I don't understand the 'we.' Where was he when I was out there freezing my butt off?"[4]

ANITA DeFRANTZ, Olympic rower

Most Americans, no matter how talented, would never be able to go the Olympics anyway. U.S. international champions generally come from just two sections of the population—upper middle-class whites and poor blacks. There are obvious reasons for this.

One is the continuing discrimination against blacks and other minorities in sports such as swimming, gymnastics, and figure skating. And even if there were an attempt to integrate these sports, few minorities would be able to participate in them because of the cost of equipment and training.

Only the wealthy can afford the tremendous costs of the training required to produce Olympic-caliber athletes in sports such as swimming. (There is certainly no help from the government or the networks and their advertisers who eventually profit from the athlete's skill.) Only the wealthy can afford to move across the country so the son or daughter may train with a certain gymnastics or swimming coach. While this "method" cannot compete forever with the mass-based programs of the socialist countries, it is still fairly effective in certain sports.

On the other hand, the social, economic, and political inequality in the United States drives millions of minority youth to work night and day to excel in sports. Despite poor facilities and programs, this process inevitably produces some fine athletes.

Of course, it isn't true that the government is totally blind when it comes to sports. If a sport is profitable, the help is there to make sure it remains so. Professional sports receive tax breaks, subsidies, and special legislation. But if you can't make somebody a profit, it's James Butts time. Butts, from Los Angeles, won the silver medal in the triple jump in Montreal. It wasn't easy. He had to begin his training at 5 AM every day because he had to work two different jobs, thirteen hours a day, to support his family. U.S. international teams have been stranded overseas or forced to sneak out the back doors of hotels because there was no money to pay the bill.

In many sports the athletes must pay their own way to competitions or they just don't go. Or they may wind up like Ed Eliason. Eliason, a carpenter from Seattle and a member of the 1972 Olympic archery team, couldn't find an athletic body willing to pay his way to the 1976 Olympic trials in Ohio. He sold his house to raise the money and then failed to make the team. Olympic long jump champion Arnie Robinson had to try to keep in shape while working on a garbage truck. Ken Patera, thought by many to be the strongest weightlifter in the history of the sport, could not find anyone to support him while he trained so he was forced to become a professional wrestler.

Perhaps I'm being too harsh. The government has managed to come up with hundreds of millions of dollars for the Olympics. It shelled out $100 million for the 1980 Winter Olympics at Lake Placid even though few of us could afford to attend. The city of Los Angeles promised to stage the first "self-sufficient" Olympiad. But as soon as they were officially awarded the 1984 Summer Games, they changed their mind and asked for $141 million from the federal government. Los Angeles will get that and more. This money doesn't go to help our athletes train or to build a broader base for the future. It lines the pockets of the contractors who build the facilities and the shady characters who organize and stage the Games. (An $800,000 Olympic insurance contract was let without bids to two nephews of John M. Wilkins, a member of the Lake Placid Organizing Committee.) The Olympic site is changed each time because it is so enormously profitable to build a new complex even through it would be enormously logical to use one of the previously built ones.

Sometimes corporations will kick in a few bucks when their tax lawyers recommend it. The problem is that they change their minds as soon as they find a better use for their money. Chevrolet cut more than $200,000 from their annual pledge to the Junior Olympic program. Chevrolet gets much more bang for the buck from the paltry $1000 scholarships it gives out at the end of the college football games. Sears refused to honor a pledge of $25,000 to the U.S. Olympic Committee until the committee agreed to boycott the Olympics.

The 1980 Olympics saw the USOC and AAU sink to a new low. They now actually sell various squads to advertisers. Anheuser-Busch bought the bobsled team. In exchange for a few sleds, it had its logo displayed during the competition. U.S. Tobacco bought the right to use the Olympic insignia in its advertising. It paid for this right with subsidies it receives from the federal government. Beer, cigarettes, and sports. It's the American way.

Thus, big corporations no longer exercise mere indirect control of sports through television advertising budgets. They buy the sports and/or the major competitions themselves. "Coors Presents the 1980 World Powerlifting Championships." Some big insurance company owns masters track and field. The corporations are now in an even better position to dictate who will compete, who will coach, and how athletes will or will not be trained. In the long run this is bound to mean even more discrimination in sports. The market these companies are after is affluent and overwhelmingly white; marketing research shows that full wallets are not opened by black, Mexican, or Puerto Rican faces on the victory stand.

The USOC helps to tighten the noose around the necks of our athletes in order to help create a more favorable investment climate. USOC official Bob Paul declared, "Amateur sports are in. They've never been in a better position to bargain for corporate support. What's wrong with it? As far as product endorsements go I would hope the governing bodies put pressure on athletes to appear in commercials."[5]

What happens to the hard-earned five dollars you give to

the USOC? One official estimated that as little as five percent of the donations filters down to the sports programs themselves. It's hard to tell where the rest goes. The AAU, for instance, eagerly accepts tax money but refuses to tell anyone what they do with it.

Amateurism

It was not until the nineteenth century that the working man had enough leisure time to seriously compete in sports. But the working athlete faced a new obstacle: the law. It was *illegal* for anyone who made a living with his or her hands to take part in athletic competition. An amateur was someone so wealthy he didn't have to work and a professional was someone so poor he had to.

"I loved the amateurs best. If I had been born rich instead of poor, I would still be fighting as an amateur."[6]

> *WILFREDO GOMEZ,*
> *world super-bantamweight champion*

Nineteenth century competitions offered cash prizes upfront, but that wasn't considered professionalism since the winners didn't need the money. The men who controlled sports had never worked a day in their lives, so perhaps it was understandable that they set down the ridiculous regulations that burden us to this day. Avery Brundage, who owned a huge construction company and a $40,000,000 collection of Oriental art, could survey a world where hundreds of millions of people go to bed hungry every night and state, "I have never known or heard of a single athlete who was too poor to compete in the Olympic Games."[7]

But if you don't need the money, it's cool to take it. U.S. equestrian (horse) athletes, all wealthy, compete for a total of over $50,000 on the annual indoor circuit but have never been disqualified for professionalism. Equestrian sports do not even meet the Olympic requirement that they be contested in at least 25 countries. Yet every four years we are treated to the sight of princes jumping bushes on their horses while sports like baseball are ignored.

The IOC upholds the tarnished ideal of amateurism for a very simple reason: to reduce costs. If there were no penalties, the athletes would be able to *openly* and *in concert* negotiate with promoters and manufacturers, which would increase their share of the take quite a bit. That might mean less money for those officials who take bribes in return for getting certain equipment adopted.

"There were actual incidents at the warm-up track where shoes were taken away from the athletes by their officials right before the competition began. It was just the kind of pressure the athletes didn't need, but the shoe companies and the officials were not concerned with people, just with their own pocketbooks."[8]
    BILL TOOMEY, *former Olympic decathlon champion*

The AAU is now willing to let athletes make endorsements but only on the condition that they get a fat fee, too. For example, marathoner Frank Shorter makes commercials for Hilton Hotels and gets paid consulting fees on the side. But Hilton must first pay off the AAU to the tune of $25,000. As long as Hilton and the AAU make big bucks, Shorter is allowed to hang around. Of course Hilton needs only one marathoner, so that's too bad for everybody else. And *nobody* seems to want to give this kind of deal to minority athletes unless they appeal to a big enough market. That is the holy altar of amateurism where so many careers have been sacrificed: the market.

Let me ask you a question. Would you go to work if you didn't get paid?

The International Olympic Committee

"We just don't want to get into the mess of democracy in the IOC. . . . it sounds weird for an American to say it, I suppose, but this undemocratic organization has worked all right so far."[9]
    DOUGLAS ROBY, *IOC member from the United States*

"Worked all right so far"...roll that around on your tongue a few times. The fact that the Olympic Games have provided so much enjoyment and inspiration has not been *because* of the IOC but *in spite of it*. IOC officials established all the nationalistic rituals which give the lie to the supposed internationalism of the Olympics. They actively cooperate in maintaining the maze of hypocritical rules which govern so-called amateur sport. The IOC has encouraged the commercialism which threatens to devour the Olympics. The IOC, which has no women members, virtually ignores women athletes. Tens of thousands of women run marathons, but the IOC has refused to approve even a 3000 meter run for 1984. They claim women "can't physically handle it." Many IOC members can hardly handle the walk from limousine to cocktail party.

Who is on the IOC? Kings, princes, archdukes, and viscounts...a landowner from Uruguay...the general manager of Shell Oil in Australia...Europe's biggest coal merchant... the treasurer of the Buenos Aires Stock Exchange...a retired Indonesian army general...the chairman of a Pakistani textile company...the chairman of the Krupp industrial empire in Germany...a commercial banker from Jamaica...a major in the Brazilian army...a sugar merchant from the Philippines. The leader of the pack is IOC Chairman Lord Killanin, an investment banker. And in this corner, from the United States, we have Douglas Roby, manufacturing executive and trustee of Detroit General Hospital. His partner in crime is Julian Roosevelt, an investment banker and member of the Naval War College Foundation.

A 1979 issue of the official IOC publication, *Olympic Review,* featured a seven-page spread on sports in Morocco. Curiously, the general population of Morocco does not seem to participate in sports. But there is a wonderful picture of the king playing golf. And we are informed that, "The Royal Family takes an active part in the management of sport, as the royal prices head numerous federations."[10]

You wouldn't expect democracy to be a high priority for such a collection of robber barons and it isn't. You must speak French or English to be a member of the IOC. There are no rules or procedures for filling vacancies or adding

members. In fact, the members of the IOC aren't required to
fill vacancies at all. When it was proposed that the presidents
of all national Olympic Committees and international sports
federations be added to the IOC in an effort to make it a more
responsive body, the silence was deafening.

It's their ball and you play their way or go home.

Fussin', Feudin', Fightin'

The United States is the only country in the world without a
single, unified sports body. The result is the sorry spectacle of
different groups of bureaucrats fighting over the rights to the
bodies and careers of young men and women. There are
several reasons for this but the biggest one is money. The more
control a particular group has, the bigger the administrative
apparatus that can be supported. That can mean a full-time
job at a high salary, trips abroad, cocktail parties, opportunities for profitable deals, etc. When has the AAU or
NCAA ever put forward a position based on principle? It's
just like Texas, Puerto Rico, and the Philippines: it's there,
they want it!

Only when we take control of international sports away
from these liars and thieves will we be able to avoid the repeti-
tion of scenes like:

- In 1979 the U.S. Wrestling Foundation, an NCAA-
  backed group, challenged the AAU in arbitration for the
  right to be the national governing body. The foundation
  won, but the U.S. Olympic Committee won't seat it because the *international* federation didn't like the decision.

- The NCAA has refused to place its allotted three representatives on the Olympic Diving Committee because
  they claim the AAU already has it stacked.

- At the 1976 Olympics, Allen Coage won a bronze medal
  in judo, the first U.S. medal in the sport since 1964.
  Despite its small-time status, judo in the United States is
  split up into three warring factions and evidently Coage
  belonged to the wrong one. After the Games, a resolution
  was introduced in the U.S. Olympic Judo Committee to
  honor Coage for his performance. It was defeated.

• The NCAA wanted nothing to do with women's sports when they were getting off the ground a decade or so ago and really needed help. But now that some women's sports are making money, the NCAA has announced plans to hold their own women's championships to compete with those of the Association for Intercollegiate Athletics for Women.

A Rulebook Is A Rulebook Except When It's Not

In sports such as soccer, basketball, volleyball, wrestling, shooting, and gymnastics, U.S. athletes are trained under different rules than those used by the rest of the world. Within our national borders, there are conflicting state regulations. In Mississippi it is okay for a high school athlete to compete on teams after the regular season; in Minnesota it'll get you busted. In 1980 U.S. high schools shifted to metric events for distance running. A wise move but...instead of having the 1500 and 3000 meter runs like everybody else on the planet, it was decided to create two new events: the 1600 and 3200. *Why?*

Future Shock

Despite the obvious love of sports in the United States, we are trying to draw to a full house in international competition while playing with a short deck. Fifty million adult Americans never exercise. Degenerative diseases caused by inactivity and obesity are approaching the epidemic stage. Physical education programs are being discontinued across the country while scores on youth fitness tests remain at the low level of 14 years ago. We have 11,000 amateur boxers; the Soviet Union has 450,000. There are 3,000 Olympic weightlifters in the United States; 500,000 in the Soviet Union. Out of 32 Olympic sports, only five are widely contested at the high school level and six at the college level.

"We got no money. We got no cooperation. We got no hope."[11]

PIOTR ROGOWSKI, U.S. Olympic Luge Coach

The Locker Room Is a Ghetto

It has become a cliche in the United States that minorities have achieved equality in sports. Is this true? Is it even *possible*? You be the judge.

> *"So many people are hiding from the truth. . . It's not a matter of being prejudiced. It's a business decision. It's like a time bomb and everyone's afraid to touch it."[1]*
> DAVE DeBUSSCHERE

Football

In 1974 Joe Gilliam, who had purposely run a slow 5.0 in the 40 yard dash so that he would not be shifted to wide receiver, had one of the greatest pre-seasons in NFL history. His reward was the starting job and in the season opener he completed 17 of 31 passes for 254 yards as the Steelers destroyed the Baltimore Colts. Against Denver the next week Gilliam passed for 348 yards in a 35-35 tie. The Steelers then beat Houston 13-7 as Gilliam completed four straight passes to set up the winning score.

By this time the inevitable criticism had begun: "Gilliam passes too much." But the Steelers' best running back, Franco Harris, was off to his worst start ever. The other running back, Steve Davis, was not nearly as effective as Rocky Bleir would be later that year for Terry Bradshaw. Bruce Van Dyke, the All-Pro guard whose blocking had been key in the

Steelers' powerful running game the year before, was hurt and then traded. In other words, *Gilliam had to pass more.* After the Steelers beat Kansas City 34-24 with Gilliam at the helm, they defeated the Browns 20-16 to move into sole possession of first place in the AFC Central. The Steelers were averaging 22 points a game, better than 20 other teams. Yet the next week Joe Gilliam was permanently benched, allegedly because the Steelers were weak offensively.

As a quarterback at Omaha University Marlin Briscoe passed for a career average of 202 yards per game and in his senior year threw 25 touchdown passes. Yet he was drafted by the Denver Broncos as a defensive back. Due to injuries he was pressed into service as a quarterback in his rookie year. In his first game, he went 17 for 30 for 237 yards and three touchdowns. He directed touchdown marches of 80, 90 and 87 yards. He did not start the next week but came into the game when the Broncos were trailing 14-0 and guided them to a 21-14 win. This wasn't enough to get him into the next game but two weeks later he did start when Steve Tensi was injured. He passed for four touchdowns and 335 yards as the Broncos pulled it out 34-32. Due mainly to a porous defense, the Broncos lost their last three games. But Briscoe passed for 218 yards in one game and 251 yards and two touchdowns in another. The Broncos' response to such a fine season was to give Briscoe his outright release. He never played quarterback again.

When James Harris was with the Bills, they refused to give him a playbook. As a Ram, Harris won 20 out of 24 games he started and was named Most Valuable Player in a Pro Bowl. It wasn't good enough. When he riddled Miami's fine secondary for 437 yards, all the TV sports announcers could talk about was how he couldn't throw short. Although Harris was the leading passer in the NFC in 1976, he was traded away by the Rams for a couple of draft choices.

Outstanding black college quarterbacks who were shifted to other positions in the pros *without a trial* include Harold Bailey, Tony Dungy, Ken Riley, Willie Wood, Freddie Solomon, Nate Rivers, and Derrick Ramsey. In a modern version of the underground railroad Condredge Holloway, Warren

Moon, and Chuck Ealey have had to go to Canada to play quarterback.

These black NFL players were star quarterbacks in high school: Neal Colzie (he led Coral Gables, Florida to a national championship), Lawrence Williams, Ken Burrough, Ronnie Coleman, Earl Thomas, Sherman Smith, Dave Brown, Gene Washington, Tony Hill (he broke Gene Washington's passing records at Long Beach Poly), Harold Carmichael, Clifford Brooks (All-State at Dunbar, Texas), Jesse Green, Charles Phillips (All-CIF at Pasadena Blair), Don Woods, and Lynn Swann.

It is much easier for a white quarterback not only to play his position but also to stay in the league. In his first nine years Bobby Douglass had a completion percentage of only 42.9 and threw twice as many interceptions as touchdowns. He started for three different teams. Kim McQuilken hung on for years even though he completed only 39 percent of his passes and threw *nine times* as many interceptions as touchdowns.

Bert Jones, Kenny Stabler, Bob Berry, Joe Ferguson, Gary Huff, Bob Avellini, Jim Hart, Mike Phipps, Lynn Dickey, Terry Bradshaw, Ron Jaworski, and Joe Reed were all given plenty of playing time to develop even though their performances in the first season or two ranged from poor to unimaginably horrible.

Discrimination in pro football is certainly not limited to quarterbacks. There are *no* black placekickers in the pros, although there have been plenty available to choose from. Lonnie Perrin of the Broncos holds the Illinois high school field goal record of 52 yards. There is only one black punter in the NFL, Greg Coleman of the Vikings. He got into the league with the Browns, but only when top draft pick Tom Skladany refused to sign a contract. After Coleman had the greatest rookie coffin-corner record in pro football history, the Browns cut him. By definition, every segregated black high school or college with a football team has a black placekicker. What happens to them? Do they all become doctors or congressmen?

There is not a single black head coach or even offensive or defensive coordinator in the NFL. Eddie Robinson of

Grambling has the second-best record among active college coaches and he has produced more pro players—*one hundred and sixty*—than anyone else in history. While proven losers like Abe Gibron and Charley Winner always find work, nobody has ever even offered Eddie Robinson a special teams job.

"I really love what I'm doing at Grambling. But I would at least like to have had the opportunity to turn down a job. Every white coach in the country with my tenure has had that opportunity."[2]

EDDIE ROBINSON

Composition of the NFL by Position

	Black	White
All players	44.5	55.5
Center	2.0	98.0
Guard	25.3	74.7
Offensive Tackle	32.3	67.7
Tight End	49.4	50.6
Wide Receiver	69.0	31.0
Quarterback	5.0	95.0
Running Back	70.6	29.4
Defensive End	56.5	43.5
Defensive Tackle	42.0	58.0
Linebacker	27.5	72.5
Defensive Back	69.7	30.3
Punter	3.6	96.4
Coaches	3.8	96.2
Owners	0.0	100.0

Those positions which require handling the ball on every play (center and quarterback) are almost always played by whites. So are those offensive positions which require pulling and the reading of defenses (center, guard, tackle). Those defensive positions thought to require only strength and speed (end, tackle, nose guard) are mostly played by blacks. The defensive player regarded as merely quick (safety, corner-back) is usually black while the defensive player who calls the signals (linebacker) is usually white. Those players who have all the attention in the stadium focused on them (quarterback, punter, placekicker) are almost always white.

One reason that blacks are kept out of leadership positions in football is to try to prevent any widespread recognition and acceptance of the leadership role that blacks, and especially black workers, are playing in society as a whole. For example, in 1978 blacks voted 93 percent no on a Missouri initiative to pass a "right-to-work" law. The total vote was 40 percent yes and 60 percent no.

Pro football is followed intensely by tens of millions of people, black and white. If teams were truly integrated and some of them led by blacks, many of these fans would undoubtedly raise the broader question of why this couldn't be done in the country's economic and political life. Here we must face a few facts. While professional sports are really insignificant as investments for the corporations which own them, these same interests will not allow anyone to mess with their carefully constructed system of inequality. In 1974 black families earned only 61 percent of the average income for a white family. This totals up to $24.6 billion in extra profit for the common corporate employers of blacks and whites. A star black quarterback in the NFL could become another Muhammad Ali. While many of us may have forgotten how Ali united blacks and whites against the war in Vietnam, General Motors and U.S. Steel recall it quite well.

Many people don't share this analysis of apartheid in pro football and one of them is NFL Commissioner Pete Rozelle, the man who refused to allow a moment of silence to be observed in memory of Martin Luther King at the 1978 Super Bowl. He once said: "Many of your Negro football players have not had the early football training that the white boys had..."[3] And then he went on to explain that as more and more black athletes attend major schools they will have the proper training to play positions like quarterback. Only so wise a man as Mr. Rozelle can understand how such white quarterbacks as Dan Pastorini, Ken Anderson, Terry Bradshaw, Jim Hart, Greg Landry, Phill Simms, Cliff Stoudt, and Ron Jaworski made it to the NFL after receiving such poor training at the small schools they attended. Even more amazing is the fact that there are some *437 untrained players in the NFL who went to small schools*. How did they do it?

For better or worse, football is a violent sport in a violent society. But violence in football is not limited to hard hits by Jack Lambert or Jack Tatum and violence against blacks isn't limited to the murder of young children in Atlanta. In November 1978 James Cuba, who is black, was the starting tailback at DeKalb (Texas) High School. One day at practice Cuba was ordered to the locker room for an alleged lack of hustle. He threw his helmet to the ground and turned his back. As soon as he did, he was tackled from behind by two coaches. The fall broke James Cuba's neck and almost killed him. On September 28, 1979 two Boston high schools, Charleston and Jamaica Plain, met on the football field. That night Darryl Williams, a fifteen-year-old black from Roxbury, started his first varsity game for Jamaica Plain. A wide receiver, he caught a touchdown pass to give his team a 6-0 halftime lead. As Darryl and his teammates huddled along the sidelines at the beginning of the second half, shots rang out and Darryl crumpled to the ground, critically wounded.

Baseball

Baseball??!! Surely our national pastime is integrated. Well...things have changed since Jackie Robinson *rebroke* the color bar in 1947. *Rebroke* the color bar? Yes. Robinson was not the first U.S. black to play in the majors. During the Reconstruction period that followed the Civil War several blacks made it to the big time. But the end of Reconstruction was the end of them. They were driven from baseball by terror and boycotts. From that time until 1947 the only way a black could play was to pass himself off as a Cuban, which many did. Jackie Robinson was allowed to make it in 1947. It could not have happened in 1927 nor could it have waited until 1967. There is no way to understand what really went down in 1947 without understanding why there was segregation in the first place. Let's check it out...

Cotton, the basis for industrial development in the United States and throughout the world, had to be grown and harvested by slaves. No one would *willingly* labor in the malarial, snake-infested swamps of the Black Belt when there was land for the taking down the road on which you could grow your own cotton. It was the tremendous amount of un-cultivated land in the United States that made slavery and segregation inevitable.

The Civil War brought an end to formal slavery and also saw the emergence of a handful of black baseball stars. Reconstruction was in reality the manipulation of the gigantic struggles for land and democratic rights by both ex-slaves and poor white farmers. They were used as pawns by Northern bankers to break the still-considerable power of the defeated slaveowners. With blacks allowed to vote and even elected to office, it was inevitable that a similar limited integration of baseball would take place. But once the Wall Street interests had captured the South they had no further use for the facade of freedom. It was quickly dismantled in an orgy of terror in which the Ku Klux Klan was born and developed. At the same time blacks were also driven out of baseball. In fact, the feet-first slide was developed at that time as a device to maim black infielders. Constitutional amendments notwithstanding, the segregation and total isolation of blacks continued after the Civil War.

By 1927, 55 percent of the world's cotton still came from the Black Belt where it was grown by unpaid labor. Just like today's South African diamond mines, these cotton planta-tions were very unproductive and inefficient but turned a handsome profit because the labor was essentially free. This is the real basis for segregation by color in the United States: the drive for maximum profit. Businessmen merely make use of whatever divisions among the people history has made it possible for them to exploit. In Ireland, it's religion; in the United States, it's color. During this period black baseball stars such as Satchel Paige and Cool Papa Bell shone brightly in the Negro Leagues without a snowball's chance in hell of reaching the majors.

But by 1940 cotton-picking machines were on the horizon and blacks had to be gotten off the land to make way for the development of huge, mechanized plantations. In addition, the depletion of Southern soil, the boll weevil, the growth of war industries in the North, and the rapid expansion of Southern industry to produce for the Marshall Plan combined to create one of the greatest mass migrations in history. In just nine years four million people left the rural South. At the same time a young man named Jackie Robinson was honing his skills at the University of Southern California.

So we arrive at the year 1947. Millions of blacks are concentrated in cities and industry. The South needed to be industrialized but it was virtually illegal for blacks and whites to work together. This situation was intolerable to Northern investors. The federal government could not continue to wear the cloak of freedom's champion while openly enforcing Jim Crow. Changes had to be made and were made. Jackie Robinson didn't have to play in the majors and Rosa Parks didn't have to get on the bus, but somebody had to.

By 1960 12 percent of all major leaguers were black; by 1968 this had risen to 22 percent. But once again the winds shifted. By 1977 only 16 percent of major leaguers were black. Five years ago over 30 percent of all minor leaguers were black but that figure has fallen to 15 percent. There was only one black player on the 1980 *Sporting News* college baseball All-American team; there were none in 1979. Even black participation in Little League is declining. The percentage of black major league players will continue to fall.

As in football, blacks in baseball are not allowed to play just any position. The players who handle the ball and must think on every pitch (catcher and pitcher) are almost always white. The outfield supposedly requires only speed and a strong arm and thus has become the traditional ghetto. While there are plenty of black Latin Americans at the key position of shortstop, you will almost never find a black from the United States there. This led Roberto Clemente to remark: "It just goes to show you how crazy the question of race is in America. If you speak Spanish you're somehow not as black."[4]

Percentage of U.S. Blacks in Baseball by Position and Year

Position	1960	1968	1977
Pitcher	3	9	5
Catcher	11	12	4
First Base	17	40	21

Other Infield	11	23	10
Outfield	24	53	44
Manager	0	0	0
Owner	0	0	0

Frank Robinson is still the only black man to manage a full season in the majors. Did he get a fair chance? The day after he had an argument with pitcher Gaylord Perry that made newspaper headlines, a huge banner hung in Cleveland Stadium that read "Sickle Cell Anemia: White Man's Hope." While he was subjected to pressures no man before him had faced, Robinson guided the Indians to their best two-year record in a decade. He was fired. True, the Indians did not set the world on fire. But *41 times* since World War II managing jobs have been given to whites with worse records than Robinson's. Two of these hacks were awarded the helms of five different clubs although they never produced a single winning season.

Even the players from the old Negro Leagues are still discriminated against. After they had been barred from the Hall of Fame for years, they were finally allowed into a special segregated section but a quota of only nine was set. There is a tired old argument that the players from the Negro Leagues were not as good. The fact that will not go away is that they won sixty percent of their games against major league all-stars.

The beat goes on. In the 1978 Hall of Fame balloting the best any black player could do was eleventh (Maury Wills, who changed the game single-handedly). Out of 31 players who received votes, 27 were white. Nearly two dozen writers voted *against* Willie Mays' induction in 1979. To check on Latin Americans in the Hall, I called the public relations man at Cooperstown. I asked him if it were really true that Roberto Clemente is the only Latin major leaguer in the Hall of Fame. "Oh no," he said. So I asked him for the names of the others. He was silent for almost a minute and then said he would have to look them up. Five minutes later he came back on the line and reluctantly admitted that Clemente was the only one.

No surprise. It wasn't until 1978 that a Latin American (Manny Trillo) was elected a team captain. There is a *legally established quota* for Latin players on major league teams which can be exceeded only with the written permission of the Immigration and Naturalization Service. How could it be otherwise when the corporations and the government manipulate the flow of Latin Americans into the United States like a yo-yo? The restriction in baseball is there to prevent an overzealous front office from concentrating only on winning by using too many Latin stars. The poverty-stricken Latins in the United States are not the market that professional sports is designed to exploit.

Despite such restrictions, does anybody really believe that Clemente is the only Latin major leaguer who should be in the Hall? Yes. In fact, there is a large group of such people: the sportswriters who select the inductees. As long as that profession remains segregated, so will Cooperstown.

Why do Latin Americans have to come to the United States to play ball? They have enough good players and enthusiastic fans to set up their own leagues. I know I used to wonder about it until I got a chance to see some of the Mexican countryside courtesy of the U.S. military. The obvious reason is the poverty, poverty made worse by the fact that so much of the wealth generated in Mexico flows north to U.S. investors. A Mexican worker at General Motors' wiring harness plant in Juarez, Mexico makes $8 a day. He certainly can't afford a box seat and he can't afford most of the products that sports help to sell.

Basketball

Yes, the NBA is 71 percent black and blacks are well represented at all positions. Yes, but... First of all, the positions people play in basketball are determined by their height more than in any other sport. In other words, you might be able to take a quick black quarterback and exile him to wide receiver, but you can't just take a 7 foot 3 inch center and play him at guard. You would never know from watching a football game if a defensive back could pass or from a baseball game if the first baseman could pitch. But in basketball everyone can clearly see all facets of a player's game: shooting, rebounding, defense, ballhandling. It's impossible to segregate basketball players by position. The "solution" used to be to keep blacks out of the pros altogether. And so it was until the 1950s when the NBA began to "integrate." Since then the number of black players has continued to rise but not without a continual struggle over quotas. How many blacks can start at home? How many on the road?

"San Antonio apparently could have had Cleveland's Mike Mitchell even up for Mark Olberding, but the Spurs reportedly turned down the deal because they didn't want to part with their last white starter . . ."5
SPORTING NEWS

I am going to come right out and say it. The NBA is segregated *against* blacks. Not just because so few black fans can afford to attend the games (black family income is now only 57 percent that of white families). Black *players* are kept out of the NBA solely on account of their color. There is a city-by-city quota system. The result is that the whiter the city the whiter the team. Phoenix has the smallest black population and the most white players. In Phoenix, Portland, San Antonio, San Diego, Denver, and Milwaukee the black population is less than 15 percent. The NBA teams in those cities have 13 percent more whites than the league average. The coaches don't pick the team; the market does.

"Realistically, I sure as hell think the white guy has a better opportunity."6
DAVE DeBUSSCHERE

"The unwritten rule now is that there should be a minimum of three white players on each team."7
LENNY WILKENS

"There are a number of players in the NBA who are on teams not because of their ability but because they're white. It's a problem. There is also the problem—expressed by both black

and white players—that there are too many black players and that this could adversely affect television viewing and game attendance. But what's the solution? Nobody knows."[8]

LARRY FLEISCHER,
NBA Players Association Counsel

"The fairest way to put it is, if a black and white player are equal, I think the white player would get the edge in time played and pictures in the program."[9]

AL McGUIRE

"...when I go in with a fringe player who's white, I can squeeze out a little more money."[10]

IRWIN WEINER, agent

Reverse discrimination, anyone?

Still the question remains. Why is the percentage of blacks higher in basketball than in any other sport? Mainly for the same reason it is disproportionately high in any sport that blacks are allowed to play. In our major cities the unemployment rate for black youth ranges between 40 and 75 percent; 39 percent of all black youth live below the official poverty level. Only two percent of General Motors' skilled tradesmen are black. Black youth are well aware that one of their very few chances for a decent life is through sports. You might as well pass a law: blacks have to try harder to make it in sports.

"I remember when I was about twelve years old, I'd go over to my school, P.S. 68 on 128th Street, in the wintertime and shovel away the snow so I could use the court...I shoveled snow, I played in the rain, I never stopped."[11]

BOBBY HUNTER, former Globetrotter

Another factor that brings basketball to the fore is that the slums where many blacks are forced to live have bad schools with worse facilities. It is no accident that few, if any, great football players have come out of Harlem or the Southside of Chicago. Where would they play? Where would their schools get the money for all that equipment and half-a-dozen coaches? Their own meager reserve of tax dollars is taken from them and given to the suburban school districts. Yet it is an easy thing to put up a hoop somewhere and other equipment costs for basketball are slight.

"The white high school had all the best equipment and books and our school had no science lab. I thought I was okay because I did well in what we had. But then I got to college and found that I wasn't prepared. There was no way to know that in Georgia."[12]

WALT FRAZIER

Seventy-one percent of the NBA is black...Phil Hankinson was a star for Penn in the early 1970s. All-Ivy League. His team won big. He was drafted by the Celtics but tore up his knee. Tried to come back but got cut. Today he's pumping gas in South Carolina.

Seventy-one percent of the NBA is black...So what?

"Sure there are good players here, and good ones who have made it in college or the pros. But don't try to write this up as a beautiful breeding ground for future stars, because for every star you hear about, there are many more who never escaped. I mean, I can look back on the group I grew up with on 111th Street, and I can tell you about the one or two who are playing college ball and it will make a great story. But there were twenty of us. And now maybe fifteen of us are on drugs and three are dead or just gone. So how much do the lucky ones count?"[13]

HARLEM PLAYGROUND PLAYER

Track and Field

In track and field the sprints, jumps, and hurdles are for American blacks, the long distances are for African blacks, and everything else is for whites. How does this happen?

It is possible to sprint and jump, although with great difficulty, in the shabby ghetto schools with their poor or non-existent facilities. But facilities for field events cost money and require space, which requires even more money. A portable landing pit costs about $2500. There is little money available to hire top coaches or train the ones on hand.

Strength events require extensive weightlifting programs. This means a weight room and the proper diet. Meat, cheese, fresh fruit, and fresh vegetables are seldom-seen delicacies to millions of American minorities. Upper middle-class athletes, who are overwhelmingly white, are often even able to have themselves videotaped and then get their form broken down inch by inch and analyzed by computer. Many inner-city high schools can't afford *any* track program at all and the track athletes must run for small clubs that have to beg, borrow, and steal just to scrape together the gas money to get to a meet.

Often the coach (who is white 99 times out of 100 above the high school level) helps to channel blacks into the hurdles and dashes in the mistaken belief they cannot excel at anything else.

If I'm wrong, then how do you explain the fact that in this country track events are segregated as rigidily as if it were required by a Constitutional amendment?

One of the surprise success stories of the past decade has been the East African distance runners. They have overcome tremendous obstacles to win countless championships. In East Africa itself, higher education barely exists and the few universities there cannot afford to give out track scholarships. In Kenya there is not a single artificial track and only one track club.

Fifteen years ago this meant nothing in the United States. Everybody knew that "blacks can't run distances," and we had plenty of world class black sprinters at home. "Scientific studies" in the tradition of Nazi Germany's Dr. Joseph Mengele were carried out to prove that "excessive tendon length" or "heavy body density" were the reasons that all blacks could do was sprint and jump. But at the 1968 Olympics this nonsense evaporated as several East African runners won gold medals. The trend has continued. In 1978 Henry Rono of Kenya obliterated the world records for the 3000, 5000, 10,000 and steeplechase. The winner of the 5000 and the

10,000 at the 1979 World Cup was Miruts Yifter of Ethiopia.

The real bone of contention today is not whether or not blacks can run distances. (Oh, how quickly those "scientific studies" disappeared.) Today the issue is whether African blacks should be allowed to run at all in the United States.

For years U.S. college track coaches have signed African athletes to scholarships and they are a powerful factor at every championship meet. The coaches who have not signed Africans have lobbied for rule changes that would keep them out of competition. Most vocal is UCLA coach Jim Bush. His position can be summed up in the time-honored slogan "Send them back to Africa!"

It's interesting that this controversy arose only when *Africans* began to get track scholarships. Irish and British runners have won college championships here for 25 years and nobody said a word. It doesn't seem to bother anybody that more and more Scandinavian weightmen are making their presence felt in the United States. Say it ain't so, Jim Bush.

Also overlooked is the "special attention" African athletes in the United States often get from their coaches. They have been threatened on many occasions with deportation if they don't do as they're told, if they don't run in every meet that comes along.

"Africans are afraid to stand up for themselves, afraid they will be thrown out and made to go home if they don't turn out as often as they're told."[14]
        ROBERT OUKO *of Kenya and North Carolina Central*

What lies behind the attitude towards Africans and the very different attitude towards Europeans? It would be easy to chalk it up to skin color but that is merely a symptom. The basis for the problem lies in the relationship between the United States and the various countries of the world. Most African countries are economic colonies of the U.S.-led Trilateralist financiers. A section of the incredible profits squeezed out of Africa (and Latin America, Asia, and the South) have gone to buy the silence of U.S. labor by providing a very high standard of living for millions of U.S. workers.

How else can you explain the difference between the standard of living of an autoworker in Ohio and that of an autoworker in South Africa, both of whom do the same job for the same company? To insure that the American people would doze in the sun while the multinationals and the CIA looted Africa, it was necessary to encourage the idea that people of color were inferior and that their conditions of life were of no consequence. On the other hand, European countries enjoy a very different economic relationship with the United States. They have their own extremely profitable investments in Africa and the Middle East and in fact have billions of dollars invested in the United States, especially in the South. Thus, Swedish hammer throwers are welcome and Kenyan steeplechasers are not.

White Man's Disease

Many sportswriters spend their spare time identifying the victims of "white man's disease" (John Doe is slow or can't jump). Are whites really slower than blacks? Can blacks jump higher than whites? No, no, a thousand times no.

Let the jury ponder the evidence:

- All medal winners in the 100 meter dash at the 1960 Olympics were white.
- David Thompson of the Denver Nuggets has a 48″ vertical jump but so does Alexander Savin of the Soviet national volleyball team. Several white members of the U.S. national volleyball team can put their necks even with a basketball rim. Greg Joy of Canada, high jump silver medalist at the 1976 Olympics, has a vertical jump of 60″.
- Allan Wells of Scotland has run a 10.07 100 meters without starting blocks.
- Valeri Brozov won both the 100 and 200 at the 1972 Olympics and holds the European 200 meter record of 20.00. Pietro Mennea of Italy holds the world 200 meter record of 19.72.
- In 1978 Wayne Johnson captured the Texas High School AAAA championship in both the 100 and 200. He is white.
- The U.S. high school 400 meter record (automatic timing) and the world 300 meter dash and 400 meter dash (indoor) records are held by whites.

This is not to deny the great achievements of blacks in the sprints and jumps, nor to deny that blacks in the United States and the Caribbean have been much more successful than whites in certain events. But the cause of this disparity is not some imaginary difference between races; it flows from the dynamics of our unequal society. Check this out:

Fifteen Deep World Rankings (1977):
100, 200, 400, 110 Hurdles, 400 Hurdles

American blacks	38
Non-American whites	24
Non-American blacks	12
American whites	1

If blacks *are* faster, what makes them so? Describe to me a world class black sprinter. You can't do it. He might be short and stocky like Mel Pender, Houston McTear, or Clancy Edwards or he might be tall and lanky like Steve Williams or Tommie Smith. There are just as many differences among black athletes as there are between blacks and whites.

"I've heard people with the explanation about the length of the lower leg or the tendon or the Achilles or whatever... You go down to the black community to talk to them or their boys club or their YMCA, and those kids are out there eight, ten, twelve hours a day, practicing! They work at it harder because it's their way out. When I go to a group where white parents and kids are gathered, after my little talk, when it's question and answer period, they ask questions like: What's Unitas like? What kind of plays did you run against the New York Jets? Why didn't Earl Morrall throw the ball? All those questions. When I go to a black function, these kids raise their hands and ask: How much money do you make? How much does John Unitas make? How do you make it in professional athletics? What do you have to do to be good enough? How fast do you have to run? What do I have to do to get up there and get out of here?"[15]

BILL CURRY, *Georgia Tech football coach
(former All-Pro center)*

Golf

John Shippen, a black man, was the first U.S.-born professional golfer and finished fifth in the inaugural U.S. Open. But shortly after Shippen's 19th century debut, the professional golf tour was restricted to "Caucasians." That ban was not lifted until 1962. But few minority families can afford the exorbitant greens fees or the motorized carts now mandatory on many courses. There are no golf courses in Bedford-Stuyvesant, East Los Angeles, or the Southside of Chicago.

Even if you have the money and a way to get there, that still may not be enough. Willie Lanier, the All-Pro linebacker of the Kansas City Chiefs, moved right next door to a country club in Richmond, Virginia so that he could play golf easily. But he wasn't allowed to join because he is black.

Etc., Etc.

The costs of competition, training, and travel in many sports are as effective in eliminating minorities (and indeed the vast majority of whites) as a Constitutional amendment. It costs at least $15,000 a year to maintain a world class figure skater, $6,000 for a gymnast, $3,000 for a swimmer or weight-lifter.

Minorities are forced into boxing just to survive. Featherweight Danny Lopez was raised on a Ute Indian reservation in Utah. He grew to his small size on a diet of powdered eggs and sugar sandwiches. Joe Frazier saw four brothers and sisters die from malnutrition back home in South Carolina. But the forces of the market are always at work. Promoter Don King declared, "I'd run through the jungle and fight a lion with a switch to get a good white fighter."[16]

Owners, who don't do any work that I am aware of, are never characterized as lazy. That distinction is reserved for minority ballplayers. It reached a fever pitch with Clemente and has yet to subside.

J.R. Richard was the workhorse of the Houston Astros pitching staff. He didn't miss a start for five solid years. On June 17, 1980 he began to experience a deadness in his pitching arm during a game with the Cubs. He sat out eleven days and all of a sudden his five years as a regular starter were forgotten. The Houston media launched a vicious campaign of hate and innuendo against Richard ("Who Shot J.R.'s Arm?") and even some of his teammates joined in. They made it clear they thought he was dogging it.

From the end of June until the middle of July Richard pitched only a couple of times, never lasting more than a few innings. The press ridiculed him for not being willing to "play with pain." On July 23 tests revealed a blood clot in his arm. The team doctors decided that it should not be operated on, since they hoped that Richard would be able to pitch during the stretch pennant drive. Well, they were wrong. On July 30 J.R. Richard had a stroke and almost died while working out at the Astrodome. No one knows if he will ever pitch again.

Rod Carew summed up this sick phenomenon when he talked about the career of Tony Oliva: "Tony never got the acclaim he deserved, and I learned what you have to do by being around him. On the road he'd carry a big brown suitcase filled with electric massagers for his knees. They were awful. I'd hear him crying in the night from the pain. Yet people didn't believe he was suffering. A typical Latin, dogging it, complaining, they'd whisper. Well, Oliva played until he couldn't walk. He ruined his health and lost his livelihood trying to live down the lies and rumors."[17]

The Pot Is Hot But It's Not Melting

What about Mexicans, Puerto Ricans, Indians, Filipinos, Hawaiians, and others? For all intents and purposes, they are excluded from the upper levels of sport. You can't write about Puerto Ricans in the NBA when there aren't any. You can't write about the problems of Navajos in gymnastics when none ever get a chance to chalk up. What it boils down to is that blacks have been allowed a distinctly limited level of "success" in sports which has been denied to other minorities.

It's true that the people who have recently arrived here have a different sports tradition and different interests such as soccer and kickboxing. But unless a sport can be marketed profitably, the interests of the "immigrants" (the Indians, Mexicans, and Hawaiians were here first) will not be provided for. Even when a "foreign" sport does become an attractive investment, the people who made it what it was and brought it to the United States are frozen out. Soccer is the most popular sport in the world; but until recently it was not a big deal in the United States, both for historical reasons and because established pro sports leagues didn't want any competition for the immense American market. It was kept alive here mainly by Latin Americans and southern Europeans. But now that soccer is popular in the United States, the professional leagues have set quotas for how many "foreigners" can be on the teams. They want to sell season tickets to corporations as tax write-offs and promote products to the upper middle class. Thus, markedly inferior domestic players fill out the rosters in order that multinational corporations can satisfy their stockholders.

Still, can it really be true that blacks have been allowed to succeed where others have been left out? This would seem to fly in the face of nearly four hundred years of history. Like so many other perplexing questions about the United States, the answer can be found in the South.

Tremendous amounts of capital were accumulated during World War II by Wall Street financiers who needed outlets for it as soon as the war was over. They chose to invest hundreds of billions of dollars in the South where they wouldn't be annoyed by things like unions or the Constitution. Yet it was impossible to set up modern production facilities when blacks and whites were not allowed to work together. Thus a certain sector of the business community and their representatives in government supported the historic struggle of blacks for equality but only to the point that it allowed for efficient exploitation of the South. Under such circumstances, the right-wing general in the White House had to send federal troops to Little Rock to insure school integration and it was impossible to keep blacks from breaking down some of the color barriers in sports.

Run It Back

Despite the millions of words that have been written on the

subject of discrimination in sports, despite thousands of protests, despite the heroic efforts of people in the schools, the gyms, and on the playgrounds, discrimination in sports gets worse with each passing day. Sports reflect the economic base of society like a mirror reflects your face. It isn't just a pack of bigoted coaches, owners, and fans, although these people certainly do exist. The real answer is found in the $25 billion bonus that discrimination against blacks represents to business and even that figure is only the tip of the iceberg. The contributions of all the other underpaid minorities to the corporate accounts must be figured in. Southern whites, who average $2000 a year less than Northern blacks, kick big bucks into the pot every time the corporate ante is raised. Add in the extra billions that segregated minorities must pay for the necessities of life and the way that the wages of whites are securely held down by the position of minorities and you begin to realize just how much is at stake.

Sports aren't any different because in this country sports are just another business, another tax shelter, another bottom line. Pete Rozelle and George Steinbrenner welcome the inequality in sports as well as in society as a whole because it serves them quite well.

"The Lions, when I was personnel director, they practically ordered me to draft more colored guys than white guys. You know why? Cheaper, they sign cheaper."[19]
                                        CARL BRETTSCHNEIDER

Segregation began with slavery for just one reason: profit. Today the traditional Black Belt area is nearly as segregated as it was 200 years ago. It remains one of the most profitable and politically stable areas in the entire world for investment. Germany, Japan, Brazil, and even Taiwan have sunk billions of dollars into the South. Equal rights in the South would put an end to this corporate paradise. Equal rights in the North would cause an uncontrollable exodus from the South and thus discrimination in the North must be maintained.

If I may answer the question I posed at the outset, no it is *not possible* for there to be equality in sports. Not as long as the South remains the way it is. Keep that in mind the next time a black player gets shot during a football game.

> Climbin' up the ladder
> I keep climbin' and I'm bound to know
> Climbin' climbin' the ladder
> Though it be shakin'
> Ain't it up that I gotta go?
>
> Keep me in the backroads
> Why should I stay down
> I keep tryin', tryin' my best now, baby
> To reach that solid ground
>
> Ain't nothin' wrong baby, ain't nothing wrong
>   in believin' in a dream
> Ain't nothin' wrong baby, ain't nothing wrong
>   though the evidence unseen*

Muhammad Ali

Muhammad Ali is without question the best-known man on the face of the earth. He can get any world leader to sit down and talk with him even though he has neither an army behind him nor any trade agreements to use as bargaining chips.

How did this come to pass? Just a little investigation will show that it was not only Ali's boxing skills and his ability as a self-promoter but also his unyielding resistance to injustice which have made him so popular.

Muhammad Ali was born Cassius Marcellus Clay on January 17, 1942 in Louisville, Kentucky. He was named after an ancestor's former master, General Cassius Marcellus Clay. The first Clay rose to the rank of general in the Civil War and was appointed U.S. ambassador to Russia by Abraham Lincoln.

One of Ali's teachers at Central High in Louisville would often say to him, "Cassius Marcellus Clay, if you could just follow in the steps of the great friend of Abraham Lincoln, that fighting abolitionist whose name you carry..." Ali put an end to such talk when he brought the book *The Writings of Cassius M. Clay* by Horace Greeley to school and read aloud, "I am of the opinion that the Caucasian or white is the superior race; they have a larger and better formed brain; much more developed form and exquisite structure..." Small wonder that later in life Ali would be only too happy to be rid of the name Cassius Clay.

Many people still don't understand how a great and wealthy athlete like Ali could refuse to join the army or why he became a Muslim. But to see where someone's coming from, you've got to look at where they've been. As All-Pro Defensive End Deacon Jones put it, "The American flag has a lot of black men's blood on it. When they sing 'Oh, say can you see' before football games, I can't help thinking how much of this country is closed to blacks and how little they get to share in its wealth and pleasures."[1]

For years after Ali won the Olympic gold medal, blacks in Louisville had to sit in the back of the bus and the Fountain Ferry Amusement Park was for whites only. The West End, where Ali was raised, and the suburb of Newburgh were the only places where a black could buy a home. Ali's former trainer Fred Stone described the scene: "Everything was segregated. The city recreation, the parks, everything...you couldn't go into a park and play tennis... You couldn't go to the golf courses to play golf. All those who wanted to, they'd have been arrested. I tell you it was so bad that every time I went to the fights I was looking to get arrested."[2]

And today? It was recently revealed that the Louisville Police Department has been thoroughly infiltrated by the Ku Klux Klan.

Although there was a strong civil rights movement in Louisville in the early 1960s, Ali was not really a part of it. He was usually on the road and many a night had to eat and sleep in his car because no one would serve him. He did take part in one demonstration and got boiling water poured on his head for his trouble. While visiting Atlanta after he won the Olympic light heavyweight title, Ali couldn't find a single restaurant that would serve him. Experiences like these led him to throw his gold medal into the Ohio River in disgust.

Despite all this, when Ali was asked by a Soviet journalist at the Olympics how it felt to win a gold medal for a country where he could not eat at the same table as a white man, he replied, "You tell your readers we got qualified people working on that...the USA is still the best country in the world."[3]

Everyone's patience has its limits. Shortly after he embarked on his professional career in 1960, Ali went to his first Muslim meeting in Miami. While he continued to fight and win, he drew closer and closer to the Muslims and became a friend of Malcolm X. By late 1962 Ali was speaking out in a manner very unusual for heavyweight boxers: "You are only free if you are Number One. Otherwise you are a slave. They say Lincoln freed the slaves. But look around you. They're still slaves..."[4]

Late in 1963 Ali invited Malcolm X and his wife to the training camp in Miami where he was getting ready for his first title fight with Sonny Liston. The fight's promoter was afraid that any connection with the Muslims would hurt the gate and declared that he would cancel the fight unless Ali denounced them. Ali told the man that under those conditions he could take the fight and shove it. Eventually a compromise was reached in which Malcolm X left the camp and Ali agreed not to make any public statements until after the fight. On February 25, 1964, the 8-1 underdog whipped Sonny Liston to become the new heavyweight champion of the world. Two days later Ali announced to the world that he had indeed become a Muslim. "I don't have to be what you want me to be. I am free to be what I want...All I want is peace."[5]

But there would be no peace. Immediately a million dollars in endorsements was lost. Ali was attacked by everybody from Joe Louis to the Governor of Maine. The World Boxing Association (WBA) threatened to take away his title. Floyd Patterson vowed to come out of retirement and "win back the title for America."

In one of history's great tidal waves of hypocrisy, the Muslims were attacked from all sides as a violent hate group. The U.S. government had invaded Vietnam but it was not attacked. The Ku Klux Klan was blowing up little children in churches yet criticism of them was mild compared to that of the Muslims. The Muslims never invaded a single country, never lynched a single person, never shot anyone for moving into a particular neighborhood. Some hate group.

On another front, 1962 saw Ali classified 1-A by the Louisville Draft Board. He was ordered to report to the Army Induction Center in Coral Gables a month before the first Liston fight. He passed the physical but failed the "intelligence" test and was classified 1-Y.

Despite the attempts of the WBA to take away Ali's title for becoming a Muslim, a return bout with Liston was set for Boston. Under pressure from various "patriotic" groups the state attorney-general refused to allow the fight. So it wound up in the unlikely venue of Lewiston, Maine. Such hysteria against Ali had been created by the press that it became necessary to search and frisk everyone who entered the arena on fight night. After he knocked Liston out in the first round, Ali prepared to face ex-champion Floyd Patterson (who had recently changed his religion with no uproar whatsoever).

On the morning of the fight Patterson was summoned to Frank Sinatra's hotel room. Sinatra "told me I could win," Floyd reported later, "[told me] how so many people were counting on me to win the championship back from Clay."[6] Floyd had the dubious distinction of being the first black "white hope" in history. "I am going to punish him," predicted Ali, and that he did. He strung Patterson along for 12 rounds while he battered him just as Jack Johnson had battered Jim Jeffries a half-century earlier. In a graphic demonstration of the real position of even the wealthiest black athlete, Sinatra refused to speak to Floyd Patterson after the fight.

By February 1966 the Pentagon needed more warm bodies and the passing score on the intelligence test was dropped 15 points. Before you could say, "Why are we in Vietnam?" two million men, including Ali, became 1-A. His response was: "Why are they gunning for me? I ain't got no quarrel with them Viet Cong."[7] Ali was accused of being a tool of Hanoi and came under tremendous pressure to retract his statement. He refused and went on to coin the famous phrase, "No Viet Cong ever called me nigger!"[8]

The price was paid immediately. A scheduled bout with Ernie Terrell in New York was stopped by the state boxing commission. It was moved to Chicago but right-wing groups there forced its cancellation. Then it was moved to Ali's hometown of Louisville but still no dice. From there the proposed fight went on tour from Pittsburgh to Bangor, Maine to Huron, South Dakota until Ali realized that, like Jack Johnson before him, he would have to leave his own country to fight. Eventually Toronto accepted the fight but then Terrell, under tremendous pressure from the FBI, backed out. So Ali wound up fighting George Chuvalo and decisioned him unanimously. Ali won three fights in Europe before he finally got two fights in Houston, where he annihilated Cleveland Williams and Ernie Terrell.

By then Ali had made it clear that he would refuse induction. This terrified the U.S. government, which did not want to help create a visible and popular symbol of resistance to the war. They offered Ali a deal. He could go overseas for awhile to entertain the troops, return to fight Floyd Patterson, and finish up his time stateside in special services. Ali refused. Under the leadership of Jim Brown and Bill Russell, many of the most famous black athletes in the United States gathered in Cleveland to urge him to accept a compromise. Ali replied: "I love my people. The little Negroes, they catching hell. They hungry. They raggedy. They getting beat up, shot, killed, just for asking for justice. They can't eat no good food. They can't get a job. They got no future. They was nothing but slaves and they the most hated people. They fought in all the wars but they live in the worst houses, eat the worst food and pay the highest rent, the highest light bill, the highest gas bill. Now I'm the one's catching hell, too. I could make millions if I led my people the wrong way, to something I know is wrong. So now I have to make a decision. Step into a billion dollars and denounce my people or step into poverty and teach them the truth. Damn the money. Damn the heavyweight championship. Damn everything. I will die before I sell out my people for the white man's money."[9]

The Army set an induction date. Ali kept on boxing while staring five years of hard time in the face. A month before the deadline he fought and destroyed Zora Folley. Angelo Dundee said later, "Cleveland Williams, that was a great fight . . . but against Folley he was fantastic. *And if he had gone on from there?* Well, there's no telling."[10]

Ali had appealed his re-classification on several grounds. After an initial rejection in Louisville he was upheld by the Circuit Court. Congressman Mendel Rivers showed his faith in our legal system when he threatened Congressional action to draft Ali if the courts did not hurry up and get on with it.

Two months later he was found guilty and sentenced to five years in prison. His words came to speak for hundreds of thousands of people inside and outside the military.

> Clean out my cell
> And take my tail
> On the trail
> For the jail
> Without bail
> Because it's better in jail
> Watchin' television fed
> Than in Vietnam somewhere dead*

Although technically he was no longer champion, Ali's supporters continued to multiply. At each of the phony WBA elimination bouts held to determine a new "champion" the chant would rise and grow..."Ah-lee, AH-LEE!" In March 1968, when Joe Frazier fought Buster Mathis for the NYAC version of the title, fight fans had to cross a picket line of anti-war, pro-Ali demonstrators. It became clear that Muhammad Ali's banishment was strictly political. The New York Boxing Commission continued to license military deserters during Ali's exile, and in 1972 even helped to secure the release of convicted murderer Ron Lyle so he could become a professional boxer.

What was Ali doing all the while? Denied the right to work in his trade while at the peak of his skills, he kept in shape anyway. He became a popular lecturer, acted a little, and like so many unemployed workers, sometimes he just drove around. "Know what I do sometimes? Drive up to Milwaukee. When I get there I turn around and come back."[11] He was signed by ABC as a commentator for a USA-USSR boxing match. Although the government put tremendous pressure on the network to keep him off the air, he did the show.

As we all remember, boxing was not the same without Muhammad Ali. It certainly was not the same for fight promoters, who longed for a return to the big paydays. But everytime they arranged a fight, the license was denied. When Ali was offered a fight in Yokohama, his lawyers asked for permission to go and promised that Ali would turn himself over to U.S. authorities upon his arrival. Denied.

*From *Holy Warrior* by Don Atyeo and Felix Dennis, p. 61.

Passport confiscated. An attempt to allow Ali to cross the border to fight in Tijuana was squashed and his offer to fight in Oakland and donate the purse to the poor in the South was ignored. ''It was impossible,'' remembered aide Gene Kilroy. ''Impossible! Hate from all sides.''[12]

But in June 1970, as U.S. troops refused to fight and the anti-war movement grew by leaps and bounds, the Supreme Court overturned Ali's conviction. After losing the best three-and-a-half years of his boxing life, Ali entered the ring again and defeated Jerry Quarry.

Since then Ali has fought brilliantly and miserably, retired (?) as the only three-time heavyweight champion in history, continued to make countless unpublicized contributions to charity, participated in a cross-country run to expose hunger and poverty in the United States, delivered an anti-apartheid address to the United Nations, made a movie about himself, and even travelled to the Soviet Union in his announced quest for world peace.

I was a scared, confused teenager humping shells in a gun mount off the coast of Vietnam when Ali began to speak out against the war. He helped me and a lot of other guys understand what was going on and saved a lot of lives. He will always have a special place in my heart.

But let's face it. Today the champ is treading water. He allowed Carter to manipulate him as a spokesman for the Olympic boycott. He has not spoken out against the reinstitution of the draft. If Ali wants to be more than a pleasant memory, he will have to once again give the forward motion of history a kick in the behind. He could use his immense worldwide popularity to focus international attention on the need to organize the South. He could help to mobilize millions to drive the Klan off the face of the earth.

The conductor is holding the train at the station. Will Muhammad Ali get on board?

The Good, the Bad, and the Might-Have-Been

Hall of Fame

ROBERTO CLEMENTE

Roberto Clemente was born in the barrio of San Anton, Puerto Rico, where per capita income was 30 cents a day and life expectancy 46. It was difficult for aspiring ballplayers to rise out of these conditions and their problems were far from over if they did make it to the mainland.

In spite of this, Clemente became one of the greatest players in baseball history. He was the eleventh player to get 3,000 hits and had a lifetime batting average of .317. He played in twelve All-Star games and won twelve consecutive Golden Glove awards. He was the National League's Most Valuable Player in 1966 and holds countless Pirate, League, and World Series records. He threw out seventeen baserunners in a single season and *once made the play on a bunt while coming in from right field*. He remains the only Latin American major leaguer in the Hall of Fame.

But during his career Clemente's greatness and his courage were not generally acknowledged. He set a Pirate record for games played although he had three ruptured spinal discs which caused constant pain and many sleepless nights. He played with stitches in his foot and with the aftereffects of malaria. Yet he was called a whiner, a hypochondriac. Roberto Clemente had as much desire and courage as any athlete. But when he felt he could not play, he sat down. That was unheard of in his day.

In 1961 his teammate Dick Groat was named Most Valuable Player in the National League. Although his batting average was eleven points higher than Clemente's, Clemente hit .310 to Groat's .214 in the World Series and drove in twice as many runs during the regular season. Clemente didn't finish second or third in the vote, he finished *eighth*. In the winter of 1964, Roberto was playing winter ball despite internal bleeding in his leg when it was announced that he had finished ninth in the race for Most Valuable Player. The second-place finisher, Johnny Callison, had an average 65 points lower than Clemente's. After the 1965 season, one of the wire services chose a major league all-star team and placed Mickey Mantle in the outfield instead of Clemente, even though Mantle had his worst year ever with a .255 average.

Clemente. . .the Latin ballplayer. . .good but never good enough.

"Roberto defended the cause of the Latins, especially the dark-skinned Latins, and they owe him a lot. Clemente wasn't a star after he got his 3,000th hit, he was a star a couple of years after he rose to the big leagues. But the press denied him the credit he deserved. I think this made him try to prove that a Puerto Rican was as good as anyone in America and could do what a Babe Ruth or Ted Williams had done. . .that in Puerto Rico, this tiny little country, there are great men, too, in every sense of the word."[1]

   PEDRIN ZORILLA, the man who signed Clemente

Clemente never lost touch with the people of Puerto Rico who, like himself, had been forced to come to the mainland to try to make a living. At Chicago's Wrigley Field there was a section of the right-field bleachers where many Puerto Ricans sat whenever the Pirates came to town. Roberto would talk to them in Spanish about things back home. One year he shared his banquet fees with Diomedes Olivo, a 40-year old rookie from the Dominican Republic who didn't have a very long career to look forward to. He once said: "I don't care if they're Puerto Ricans or not, they can be Dominican, Venezuelan, Cuban, Mexican, they're *latinos*, my people."[2]

In 1969, Clemente was 35 years old. Most men in his position would have retired. But Clemente kept going, on and off the field.

As the Pirates' player representative, he was a leader in the struggle to increase the players' pension fund out of World Series receipts.

Yet his greatest concern was for the youth of all nationalities and the problems they face as they grow up in what Muhammad Ali describes as a "freakish, vicious world." Clemente declared: "If I was President of the United States, I would build a sports city and take in kids from all ways of life. What we want to do is exchange kids with every city in the United States and show all the kids how to live and play with each other."[3]

He rejected advice to wait until after retirement to work on this sports city. Roberto understood that as soon as he quit baseball he would be "just another Puerto Rican." He was working to secure part of an old Navy base in the center of San Juan as a site for the sports city when he had to leave to begin preparation for the 1973 season.

Then on the morning of December 23, 1972 an earthquake devastated the city of Managua, Nicaragua. At least 6,000 people were killed and tens of thousands more injured or left homeless. That very night Clemente helped to formed a relief committee. He set aside his carefully laid holiday plans and threw himself into the effort. The relief drive was able to raise money and gather supplies easily. But Roberto learned that elements of the Somoza regime had diverted incoming donations for their own profit. He decided to go to Nicaragua himself, saying, "They will not steal from Clemente."[4]

An urgent request for medical supplies had been received from Managua; they were secured and loaded onto an old DC-7. On Sunday, December 31, Clemente and other volunteers loaded the plane and prepared to depart.

At 9:22 PM, as millions of people were preparing to celebrate New Year's Eve, the plane took off. It developed engine trouble as soon as it was airborne and crashed into the water about a mile off the coast. Everybody aboard was killed.

Today there are hospitals, parks, and schools across the United States and in Puerto Rico that bear the name of Roberto Clemente. Yet his fondest dream—jobs and recreation for all youth of the hemisphere—remains as distant as ever.

RICHARD PETTY

The Petty family has a long history in stock car racing and has often been involved in conflicts with track owners and track promoters. Lee Petty, Richard's father, had to fight just to be allowed to use a rollbar. Some track owners claimed that the fans would not come out unless they could see the drivers crushed to death.

In the late 1960s NASCAR drivers organized the Professional Drivers Association with Richard Petty as president. They wanted an increased share of the gate, insurance, pensions, and safer driving conditions. But NASCAR President Bill France refused to even talk about it.

When the superspeedway at Talledega, Alabama opened in 1969 it was unsafe. In practice, tires were torn right off their rims. Drivers asked France to postpone the race until the track was smooth; he refused. Some said they would not race and France declared they would not be missed.

At a meeting held before the race many top drivers wanted to pack up and leave. When Richard Petty gave the word, they did. Some did race but, as Richard said at the time, "They had a yellow flag every few laps. They were lucky they didn't have any bad accidents. But when they didn't, they said it proved we was wrong. Lordamighty, does a driver have to die before they'll do what has to be done?"[5]

GEORGE "ICE" GERVIN

"I stood in line for food with my mother in Detroit and I could have just as easily been a criminal today."[6] But GG is not just concerned with himself. Although he could make more money in a bigger city, he intends to finish out his career in San Antonio. Gervin also plans to take lessons in street Spanish so that he can better relate to the large Mexican population there. He organizes free children's clinics to "give them instructions on things I never learned on the playground."[7]

On or off the court, Ice is cool but never cold.

BOBBY HULL

In more ways than one, Bobby Hull was the best of the players who jumped from the National Hockey League (NHL) to the World Hockey Association (WHA).

The WHA was known for its recruitment of European stars but many Canadian players never accepted them. During games they slashed and hacked at the Europeans, fought and ridiculed them. Off the ice, they pressured the owners to set quotas on foreign players.

Bobby Hull couldn't stand the way his European teammates were being treated. The league wouldn't do anything about it so he took matters into his own hands. He sat out a game in protest against the violence in hockey.

When a sport's brightest star takes such dramatic action, it makes waves. Instantly a storm of criticism was directed at the WHA officials who allowed such practices.

"I've seen players who were pussycats go crazy when they'd play Europeans," said WHA senior referee Bill Friday. "Hull's protest helped because he woke up a lot of people."[8]

RICHARD LAPCHICK

Lapchick, the son of former Knicks coach Joe Lapchick, was one of the main organizers of the massive demonstrations against the appearance in Nashville of the South African Davis Cup team in the spring of 1978. Two weeks before the demonstration two men burst into Lapchick's office in Norfolk. They stabbed him and beat him severely. The local police ruled it a *suicide attempt*.

The truth came out a year later. The South African government had admitted that the two attackers were South African agents. In fact, they ranked Lapchick's near-murder as one of their top accomplishments in 1978. One question remains. Why does the U.S. government allow foreign agents to operate in this country?

ROSS MOORE

When Ross Moore began his freshman year at Ohio State, he was generally regarded as one of the finest quarterbacks ever to come out of Pennsylvania. But early that year he tore up his knee in practice and was through for the season. Following major surgery Moore came back the next year but injured his shoulder. Woody Hayes was convinced that he was "malingering" and set out to punish him. He worked him every day against the first-string defense but never used him in games. The summer before his senior year, Ross Moore got fed up and quit. In retaliation, Woody Hayes illegally took away his scholarship.

Most athletes whose futures are stolen like this keep quiet about it. They are in a weak position against a powerful opponent. They no longer make money for the university, the conference, the NCAA, or the networks. So who needs them?

But Ross Moore was lucky. He could afford to hire a lawyer and he won his scholarship back at a university hearing.

I suggest that the NCAA establish a Ross Moore Award to be given to the student or athlete each year who does the most to expose or eliminate the exploitation of college athletes.

JIM GREEN and RICHMOND FLOWERS

In the 1960s the Southeastern Conference indoor track championships were always held in Montgomery, Alabama. At these meets the Confederate flag was usually displayed instead of the Stars and Stripes.

In 1968 Jim Green, a black freshman from the University of Kentucky, and Richmond Flowers, a white star athlete from Tennessee whose home town is Montgomery, organized a petition drive among Southeastern Conference track athletes. It simply stated that they would no longer compete at meets where the Confederate flag was flown. The petition was signed by more than 120 athletes from all ten conference schools and it succeeded in bringing down the Stars and Bars.

JACKIE ROBINSON

Jackie Robinson didn't have to wait until he became a baseball player to be the target of an organized hate campaign. As a young boy he had watched his white neighbors circulate a petition demanding that the Robinson family get out of town.

So it probably didn't shock Robinson when he got to the majors and several teams tried to organize a general strike to force him out of the league. Red Treadway, a promising outfielder with the Giants, *retired* to avoid playing against Robinson.

Jackie Robinson's courage and patience in the face of constant abuse and dirty play is even more remarkable when you consider the predicament management put him in. Branch Rickey, the noble man who "integrated" baseball, told Robinson in no uncertain terms that he was expected to tolerate whatever was done to him on or off the field and come back for more with a smile.

Rickey could have made things much easier. He could have had the fans who threw things at Robinson arrested. He could have protested openly to the commissioner and the press every time a player got out of line. He could have mobilized the fans to support and defend Robinson. But Rickey just left him a sitting duck. As Robinson himself pointed out, Rickey's only motive was to attract the black fans and, of course, their wallets.

PEE WEE REESE

Pee Wee Reese was Jackie Robinson's friend and defender during a difficult and dangerous time. That first year, Robinson hit .515 in an exhibition series in Panama. Half-a-dozen Dodgers responded with a petition demanding that he not be allowed to play during the regular season. It was presented to Reese, who was expected to sign. Well-liked and respected on the team, Reese was a Southerner to boot. But he refused to sign, as did several others.

During the season, there were many times when the heckling would get particularly intense. Reese would stop play, walk over to Robinson, and put an arm around his shoulder while they talked.

THOSE WHO WOULD NOT UMP

The 1979 umpires' strike brought out the best and worst in baseball.*

*See Appendix 1.

While many minor league and amateur umpires eagerly scabbed, there were exceptions. Amateur umps Pete Lienicke and Glenn Brickey of St. Louis refused to umpire a Cards-Cubs game because they were union members. The Cleveland Umpires Association prohibited all of its members from working. Eight minor league umpires refused to move up.

There were also expressions of solidarity from other unions. The Tiger Stadium grounds crew and service employees refused to cross the picket line. Concrete support emerged in Detroit from the AFL-CIO, Teamsters, and the UAW and in Massachusetts from the state AFL-CIO council. In Pittsburgh several hundred union members picketed a "Helmet Day" game.

You don't need a degree in biology to know that a scab is the lowest form of life.

BILL RODGERS

Rodgers is one of the greatest runners in history. He has won the Boston Marathon an unprecedented three times and almost every other major race at least once.

As a college student Rodgers refused to be drafted for the Vietnam war and did alternative service as a conscientious objector. A few years later he was fired from his job at a hospital for trying to unionize the orderlies.

Today he has become an outspoken critic of the growing distortions in competitive running caused by commercial exploitation. "I'm critical of a race like Boston because major corporations are getting large amounts of commercial advertising and publicity but they still ask the runners to pay a high entry fee."

SOLID SOONERS

The town of Idabel is located in McCurtain County, Oklahoma, an area often called "Little Dixie." McCurtain County is extremely poor. Its unemployment rate is twice the state average. Black income averages only 55 percent that of whites.

On January 20, 1980 a 15-year-old black youth was found murdered, strung up on a barbed wire fence. The black community demanded an investigation. When the police refused, a riot broke out which left two people dead.

Following the riot, Ku Klux Klan leader David Wilkinson boasted that the Klan was very active in McCurtain County and that he would soon visit Idabel. The murder in Idabel, along with four others in the same area in 1979 prompted students at the University of Oklahoma to organize a large anti-Klan rally. Prominent at the rally were several members of the Oklahoma football team.

These young men put another nail in the coffin of the stereotype of the football player as a dumb jock. Whatever happens on the field, they are winners.

ONE FOR THE THUMB

In early September 1980 Klan Imperial Wizard Bill Wilkinson said on the "Tomorrow" show that the climate in the Pittsburgh area was excellent for KKK activity due to widespread steel-mill closings and busing.

Evidently, western Pennsylvania also has an excellent climate for *anti*-Klan activity. On October 25th, six weeks after Wilkinson's pronouncement, several hundred people gathered in a freezing rain in Uniontown, Pennsylvania to protest the growth of the Klan. The rally was sponsored by District 15 of the Steelworkers' Union and several other labor and community groups. Among the endorsers of the rally was the entire Pittsburgh Steeler team: from Mike Webster to Terry Bradshaw to Lynn Swann; from Joe Greene to Jack Ham to Mel Blount.

The Steelers are used to tough opponents in the AFC Central and should feel right at home battling the Klan. The outcome of that game is of vital interest to all football fans.

ERIC HEIDEN

Eric Heiden was undeniably the star of the 1980 Winter Olympics. He won five individual gold medals, an unprecedented feat. He focused worldwide attention on the obscure sport of speedskating.

But we saw what kind of stuff Heiden is really made of when he stood up to the President of the United States. Shortly after the Olympics, Heiden and several other U.S. athletes were flown to Washington to meet Jimmy Carter. Despite Carter's weeks of threats against U.S. athletes, Heiden tried to present him with an anti-boycott petition signed by over 150 Winter Olympic athletes. Carter would not accept it and refused to discuss the issue.

It is a sad commentary on sports in the United States that political hacks like Jimmy Carter decide whether or not the Eric Heidens of the future enter the Olympics.

Hall of Shame

WOODY HAYES

When Woody Hayes punched out Clemson linebacker Charlie Bauman in the 1978 Gator Bowl, it was nothing new. He always beat on his own players during practice, including 1979 top draft pick Tom Cousineau. During the 1975 Rose Bowl he hit middle guard Arnie Jones before a nationwide television audience.

In 1964 the Yankees were playing the Indians and first baseman Vic Power was having a field day picking men off. Suddenly a man charged out of the stands and tried to assault Power. The man was restrained by police and had to be ejected from the stadium. His name was Woody Hayes.

When Hayes was coaching at Denison in 1948, he kicked an opposing player who had gone out of bounds. He once hit a little boy who tried to run out on the field during a game with Michigan. He has beaten up reporters and cameramen, sometimes severely. Only in the 1978 Gator Bowl, when it was too obvious and too flagrant, was anything done about it. Only then did the hypocrites who had always protected Hayes call for his removal.

But Hayes is more than a guy with a bad temper. Always a troutmouth about democracy, he overruled his players' traditional right to elect their own captains when the vote didn't go his way. He told Jim Roseboro that he would take away Roseboro's scholarship if he didn't stay away from a band singer named Nancy Wilson (yes, *the* Nancy Wilson). Woody was one of the most ardent supporters of the Vietnam war and went to Vietnam four times to urge on the slaughter. While his career was built to a large extent off the hard work of black athletes, he himself lives in a wealthy all-white suburb of Columbus, Upper Arlington. Its composition is no accident. When a black Ohio State faculty member tried to move into Upper Arlington, he was greeted by an early morning shotgun blast.

But let Woody Hayes, the coach renowned as well read and literate, speak for himself:

- "Kenyon athletes are a bunch of intellectual effetes and Jews."[9]
- "I came to appreciate the great physical ability, rhythm, and sense of timing that black people have."[10]
- "But Nixon seems to have learned a lot since then and I think history is gonna regard him as one of our greatest Presidents, one of our greatest statesmen."[11]
- "And I told him there's an old saying about the best way to treat a woman, and that's to knock her up and hide her shoes."[12]

"That guy packs the people in. He's great for the game."[13]
DON CANHAM, Michigan Athletic Director

Today Woody Hayes keeps busy writing speeches against disarmament and busing.

HAROLD ENARSON

Winner of the Richard Nixon Honesty Award, with Peanut Leaf Cluster. As the president of Ohio State, Harold Enarson was Woody Hayes' boss. After Hayes hit Charlie Bauman, Enarson said, "There isn't a university or athletic conference in the country which would permit a coach to physically assault a college athlete."[14] Very interesting, Harold. Do you think anyone believes that you didn't know Woody Hayes hit football players all his life? What did you mean when you said that one of your major responsibilities was to defend winning football coaches?

Is it too extreme to suggest that those who allow the Woody Hayeses of this world to operate be given the boot also?

JOE DAVIS

In April 1978 the South African Davis Cup team played the U.S. team in Nashville, Tennessee. A nationwide movement to prevent the match culminated in the largest civil rights demonstration in the South in nearly ten years. Although the matches were played, the demonstration so limited attendance that the U.S. Tennis Association was forced to relieve Vanderbilt University, site of the matches, of their $50,000 guarantee.

But there was a financial angel in the wings in the person of Joe Davis, who gladly picked up the tab for his alma mater. He got the money from his own company, Davis Coals, Inc., which made a small fortune hauling non-union coal at premium prices during the 1978 United Mine Workers strike.

ALEXANDER HEARD

As chancellor of Vanderbilt, Heard refused to cancel the Davis Cup matches, citing an "open forum" policy. Moreover, he has also refused to listen to requests that the school divest itself of investments in firms that do business in South Africa. Heard is the current chairman of the Ford Foundation, which is underwritten by the Ford Motor Company. Ford has several plants in South Africa and is a strong supporter of apartheid. The starvation wages Ford pays there are an important factor in the huge foreign profits that have offset Ford's domestic losses in recent years. Vanderbilt University owns 61,250 shares of Ford Stock.

TY COBB

Ty Cobb's achievements on the field are legendary. And rightly so. What is not well known is that Ty Cobb was one of the most vile and prejudiced athletes who ever lived. Along with Gabby Street, Rogers Hornsby, and Tris Speaker, he was a member of the Ku Klux Klan. After he was charged with the unprovoked stabbing of a black waiter in Cleveland, Cobb had to avoid the state of Ohio for many years. He was the embodiment of the spirit of Cap Anson, the nineteenth century all-star who led the successful drive to eliminate blacks from baseball in the post-Reconstruction era.

MARY BACON

At one time Mary Bacon was one of the leading women jockeys in the United States. But in 1975 she became an open spokeswomen for the Ku Klux Klan. Her favorite theme was the old tired lie that all black men want to do in life is rape white women. It is to the credit of U.S. racing fans that after Bacon "came out of the closet" she had trouble finding rides anywhere in this country. Today she rides in Japan. If we're lucky she'll never come back.

DICK YOUNG

Young is the nationally syndicated sports columnist for the *New York Daily News* and the journalistic equivalent of Woody Hayes. He attacked any athlete who worked to stop the war in Vietnam or was active in the civil rights movement. He now occupies his time villifying athletes who do not exhibit the proper respect for the owners who rip them off every season. Could it be that "impartial" Dick Young has been influenced by the favors showered on his relatives by Mets owner Donald Grant?

To get the true picture of Dick Young, you have to look at a column he wrote in 1977. The subject was the Dominican Republic of 1946. Then as now, it was one of the world's poorest countries. It was ruled by General Trujillo, a Caribbean Hitler.

"It was a wonderful time and place. Trujillo said, 'Any native found stealing from Americans will be executed.' Not a baseball was stolen. When we went to the pool, we would leave money on the bed and it was all there, every last nickel, when we returned. I think of this often, whenever I hear today's bleeding hearts say that capital punishment is not a deterrent, and I remember it sure as hell was." [15]

Since two of the small number of alternatives to starvation in the Dominican Republic are stealing and baseball, perhaps General Trujillo's policies can be given partial credit for the many Dominicans who come to the United States to try to make the majors.

Halls of Fame

There is not a hall of fame in this country that does not discriminate against national minorities.

There are few blacks and only two Latins at Cooperstown, more owners than black players in the Pro Football Hall of Fame, and only a handful of blacks at the Track and Field Hall of Fame in Charleston, West Virginia.

Not even basketball, supposedly the victim of a sinister takeover by blacks, allows very many to pass through the hallowed portals of its hall of fame. In the 1979 election, Wilt Chamberlain was the only black elected.

Paul Robeson, whom Walter Camp called the greatest pre-World War I football player, has been kept out of the nearly all-white College Football Hall of Fame.

Special mention must be made of the 23 writers in the Baseball Writers of America (BBWA) who did not vote for Willie Mays in the 1979 Hall of Fame balloting. The BBWA has refused to identify these writers. If they're so proud of their baseball knowledge, why don't they step forward and speak on it? Why didn't we see columns that led off with "Willie Mays doesn't belong in the Hall of Fame and I'm proud to say I tried to keep him out...?"

GEORGE STEINBRENNER

In the spring of 1979, Steinbrenner was given the annual Leatherneck Award by the Marine Corps for his "dedication to the free enterprise system." George has done so much that it is hard to know just what it was that brought him this honor. Was it

- making illegal contributions to Richard Nixon's 1972 campaign?
- trying to force some of his employees to commit perjury on his behalf when he got caught?
- his key role in stealing one hundred million tax dollars from New York City for the overhaul of Yankee Stadium?
- paying his Yankee office staff so little they were forced to unionize?

- managing to get a one-year suspension from baseball for being a convicted felon, when the last owner in that situation was banned for life?
- continuing to interfere in the political process of the United States even though the courts took away his right to vote?
- calling Reggie Jackson "boy"?

Whatever else you might say about George Steinbrenner, you have to admit that he deserves the Leatherneck Award.

BOBBY KNIGHT

Bobby Knight is the Woody Hayes of basketball. He grabs and pushes his players during games. More good players have been driven away from Indiana than most coaches recruit in a lifetime. Knight once cancelled a game with Eastern Kentucky because they had accepted a transfer student, a basketball player.

At the 1979 Pan-American games Knight was arrested and later convicted of the assault on a Puerto Rican policeman. But even if Bobby Knight weren't guilty of assault, he should have been fired immediately for his conduct during those games. Throughout his stay as a guest of Puerto Rico, he made insulting and slanderous remarks about its people, such as, "The only thing they know how to do is grow bananas."[16]

But Bobby Knight will not be fired. Knight is a winner who brings in good money for the university and healthy profits for TV sponsors. He turns out solid pro players who sign cheap.

Hall of Broken Dreams

RAYMOND LEWIS

Unless you are one of the ten million or so lucky people who live in Los Angeles, you're probably thinking, "Raymond who?"

_____

"In Los Angeles he's a legend. You say Raymond, they say Lewis. You say Lewis, they say Raymond."[17]
          BOB HOPKINS, Knicks assistant coach

_____

Three years in a row (1969–71) he led his high school team, Verbum Dei, to the California state championship. At Cal State-LA he led the nation's freshmen in scoring with a 38.9 average and a high of 73 points. In his sophomore year he was the second-leading scorer in the country with a 32.9 average. Then he turned pro.

Or was he already a pro? When he was in *junior high school*, colleges were giving him money, clothes, and apartments. The 76ers gave him over $40,000 in cash while he was still in high school. He drove a new Corvette to classes at Cal State. His coaches got him into basket courses and his teachers never let him down. Pro agents threw money at him and gave him cars. At one point he had a Pantera, a Cadillac, and a custom van.

Raymond Lewis didn't realize he was just a way station for someone's venture capital and the sudden wealth blew his mind. He was a kid from Watts who never had anything, who had stood on the roof of his grandparents's house with a hose trying to keep away the flames during the 1965 rebellion. "The bad effect it had on me was that I tended to get soft. They were ripping me off for my talent and I slacked up. I lost a lot of motivation. It softened me and I neglected myself and my game. I was an 18-year-old with a new Corvette."[18]

In 1973 Raymond went hardship and was drafted by the 76ers. Twenty years old, he was the youngest player to be drafted and signed to an NBA contract.

In 1972 the 76ers had the worst record in the history of pro basketball, 9–73. It was a far cry from the team led by Wilt and Billy C which had snatched a championship from the invincible Celtics only a few years earlier. They needed help with a capital H but didn't want to pay for it.

Lewis *thought* he has signed a three-year contract for $450,000, but he wound up with only $55,000 a year and a $25,000 signing bonus. The 76ers' other top pick, Doug Collins, signed for $200,000 a year. At the time Doug was coming off a fine performance in the Olympics but he was basically an unknown quality. By all reports Raymond Lewis ate him alive in practice. Was the difference in salary a reflection of the difference in color between the two men?

Father Thomas James, a teacher at Verbum Dei, said,

"Those owners just laughed about the contract demands. They said, 'These niggers come all this way and tell us what *they* are going to do. *They're* telling us. We got the money and they ain't got nothing."[19]

The 76ers refused to renegotiate Lewis's contract and he began to skip practice every few days, fly back to LA, and then return. In exhibition games he did not play. After a few weeks, he was suspended. The next year he was brought back for another tryout. He walked out after two days and did not return. He made the Utah Stars in the ABA, but never played because the 76ers threatened legal action. "Raymond was not going to waltz around pro basketball doing what he wanted,"[20] declared 76er General Manager Pat Williams.

In 1978 Lewis went to the Knicks' rookie camp where he showed more than a hint of his previous greatness. He was invited back for fall camp but declined because the Knicks were loaded at guard. Instead, he signed with the San Diego Clippers. Coach Gene Shue said he played well; yet he was cut after ten days.

"Offensively, he's as good as any guard I've ever seen. He has an automatic jump shot. He's not afraid to go against anybody."[21]

BILLY PAULTZ

Raymond Lewis worked very had all his life to perfect his talent. Today he babysits while his wife works. Is this really the best our society can offer him?

FRED BUTTLER

Fred Buttler was one of the first blacks ever to attend Warren Lane Elementary School in Inglewood, California. No one could keep up with him in after-school games and he quickly established himself as a gifted natural athlete. But the real test for Fred Buttler came when the fun was over. He would run for his life with a mob of white kids on his heels and often wound up hiding in a gas station restroom.

Although Fred was an athletic standout in the fifth and sixth grades, Little League coaches refused to let him try out.

And his mother worried about his academic progress. At the end of the sixth grade she talked to his teacher and asked if he were really ready to go on to Albert Monroe Junior High School. "He's a little slow in reading," one teacher said, "but it's nothing to worry about."

As a seventh grader, Fred starred on the eighth grade football team along with a small group of other blacks who were known as the "Hersheys." Fred recalled a meeting with his teacher at the end of that year: "She sat us down in front of her big desk, smiled real nice and said how happy she was to be able to double promote all five of us to the ninth grade. We looked at each other thinking maybe she was joking. Finally Ken Carr asked if she was serious. She said, 'You're just too bright to be in the eighth grade.' Now that guy Carr couldn't read much better than me."[22]

Amazingly enough, Fred Buttler did quite well at Morningside High School. His first semester he got an A in physical education, B's in world history, math, and art, and C's in English and reading (this last grade notwithstanding the fact that he was still illiterate). How did he do it? When the tests were passed out, he would hand them in blank; they would mysteriously return all filled in and stamped with a passing grade. He seldom went to class yet graduated from high school with a C+ average. These strange happenings could have been related to Fred's standout play in the secondary. Morningside captured conference crowns in his junior and senior years.

But Fred Buttler wasn't stupid. In study hall he played chess with the best players in school and checkmated them in short order.

After he graduated 190th in a class of 355, Fred went on to play football at El Camino Junior College. Since he couldn't read the course catalogue, his coach had to help him register. Instead of placing Fred in courses that might have helped him learn to read (but might also have made him ineligible for football), the coach put him down for football, handball, basketball, weightlifting, and volleyball.

Once again the teachers cooperated as Fred led El Camino to the Metro Conference co-championship in 1972. He finished his last semester with a B+ average even though he still couldn't read about himself in the sports pages. With several scholarship offers from four-year schools, he settled on Cal State-LA after the coaches promised him they would get him into some reading courses.

When Fred Buttler arrived on campus he discovered that the coaches had lied. There were not and had never been any remedial reading courses. It was more of the same old story: golf, handball, diving. He said later: "I think some of the coaches were happy I couldn't read because that meant I wouldn't waste time on schoolwork since that way I could concentrate on playing for them."[23] And play he did. He was a star in the defensive backfield once again. "If that guy was a little bigger, he'd be drafted for sure,"[24] said a rival coach.

But Fred wasn't drafted and the chickens finally came home to roost. Cal State had no use for an illiterate black kid whose eligibility was all used up. The high-minded professors no longer saw any reason to give him a break and they didn't. Fred flunked out during winter quarter and his coaches were too busy recruiting a replacement to waste any time on him. Then he got a letter from the financial aid office. They wanted to know when he planned to pay back a $1,236 "loan" that was supposed to have been part of his scholarship.

Today Fred has moved back in with his mother. He runs a hinge-making machine at a small factory near the Los Angeles airport.

He still can't read.

FRANKIE RODRIGUEZ

Every year hundreds of thousands of Central Americans make their way to the United States in hopes of a secure future. They seldom find it.

Frankie Rodriguez came from Honduras to New York, where he became interested in boxing. On January 31, 1979 he fought as a heavyweight in the New York Golden Gloves. He was winning in the second round when suddenly he became so exhausted he couldn't continue. He left the ring and collapsed in a hallway. He died the next morning.

But Frankie Rodriguez did not die from a blow he suffered in the ring. He died from the effects of an enlarged heart and sickle cell disease, a less-advanced form of sickle cell anemia. A simple blood test might have saved his life, but none was given. Who will be next?

Three Times a Lady: Bench Press, Deadlift, Squat

One of the most radical and welcome changes in sports in the past decade has been the emergence of great numbers of women athletes. Today women compete in almost every sport, from powerlifting to rugby to water polo. In 1970 294,000 girls competed in high school sports. By 1977 that number had risen to 1.6 million. The Association for Intercollegiate Athletics for Women (AIAW) did not even exist ten years ago. Now it covers 825 schools, 115 more than the NCAA. The first women's mini-marathon in New York's Central Park drew 78 entries; by 1978 the same race had a field of over 4,300.

On the surface it would appear that women are on their way to equal opportunity in sports. Smoothly, steadily, the numbers grow. It won't be long now.

Equality would make a good story but not a true one. First of all, how can women be equal in sports when they are so unequal in everything else? In 1955 women workers made 63.9 percent of the wages of their male counterparts; today they make 58.9 percent. The median annual income for men is $14,626 while for women it is only $8,618. The average male high school dropout earns $1,604 more per year than the average woman college graduate. Women have 76 percent of the lowest-paid federal jobs but only 3 percent of the highest-paid. While women make up 14 percent of the workforce in basic industry, they hold very few union leadership positions. There is only one woman local president in basic steel and only one woman on the AFL-CIO executive council. Only 1.9 percent of the 175,000 construction trades apprentices in the United States are women. You can sum up the position of women in the United States with one fact: *this country cannot even pass a constitutional amendment which simply states that women should have the same rights as men.*

"Just the Facts, Ma'am"

But the undeniable gains that women have made in sports have created a considerable backlash which takes a variety of forms. One is opposition to girls' participation in such former all-male bastions as Little League. What this really boils down to is the question of what, if any, differences there are between the male and female of our species.

I hope we can all agree that men and women are not the same. For example:

- The male hormone, androgen, produces denser bones and more muscle mass.
- Women can lift weights without getting "musclebound" because they lack testosterone, the hormone which accounts for the muscularity of men who lift weights.
- Men have proportionately larger hearts and lungs than women, which enables them to pump more blood to the muscles. Men also have higher concentrations of hemoglobin, the substance which carries oxygen in the blood.
- At Little League age (8-12) girls are an average of two inches taller and four pounds heavier than boys.
- Girls are ahead of boys in physical development for the first ten years of life.
- There is no difference between men and women in the ability to do skilled work of mild intensity.

Do you think that due to pregnancy or menstruation women are delicate and need to be protected? Read on...

- June Stover Irwin of the U.S. won an Olympic medal in ten meter diving while four months pregnant.
- Complications of pregnancy, difficult labor, and length of labor are less for women who are active in sports. Women athletes are only one half as likely to need a caesarian section.

- Women athletes have fewer menstrual problems than non-athletes. Olympic gold medals have been won by women during all phases of the menstrual cycle.

- There have been only three known cases where women's reproductive organs were damaged through sports and those were all in water skiing.

- In a survey of 125 athletic trainers published by the American Medical Association, only 3 percent thought women were more injury-prone than men.

- More than half the Soviet women medal winners at a recent Olympics were mothers. This suggests that the problems American women have getting back in shape after childbirth are not inherent but instead are due to a lack of child care.

Second Place in a Field of Two

There it is. Men and women are not the same but the difference certainly isn't that men are strong and skilled and women are weak and clumsy. The national Pitch, Hit, and Run champion in 1979 was a girl. Batter up!

Should human beings be denied the right to participate fully in sports just because they happen to grow up without testosterone in their bodies?

In Waco, Texas the budget for boys' athletics at four senior and seven junior high schools amounts to $250,000; the girls receive only $970. In California the average high school spends $14,400 on boys' sports and $3,300 on girls'. The boys average 21 coaches who receive $505 in extra pay, while the girls have only seven who get $343.

At Captain Shreve High School in Caddo Parish, Louisiana the boys' gym suits are provided free and laundered by the school. The girls must buy their own and wash them at home. At Michigan State members of the men's teams get $16 a day in meal money and sleep two to a room on the road while the women sleep four to a room and must each make do on $11 a day.

At Springfield College, the men's swimming team gets to use the pool three hours a day while the women's team must settle for one hour. Seven-time All-American Deborah Kinney has to go to the pool at six in the morning to get in her training.

In Iowa 494 of the state's 503 high schools have girls' basketball teams. But all the coaches and administrators are men. State basketball administrator Wayne Cooley says, "We don't need women coaches or administrators to make this program work. If I hired some, they'd probably have babies in a year or two and quit, and we'd just have to start again."[1]

It was to combat such practices that Title IX of the Education Amendments was enacted by Congress in 1972. Title IX bans sex discrimination in any educational institution that receives federal funds and mandates the withdrawal of funding for non-compliance. Although Title IX regulations became law in 1975, the guidelines were so vague as to be useless. In December of 1979 specific directives for implementation were issued. The first step was supposed to be training investigators to look into complaints of Title IX violations. So far not one investigator has been trained and people who do file complaints are told to wait...and wait...and wait...

The NCAA, which banned women until 1974, has spent $300,000 of its TV money in the fight against Title IX. The National Federation of High School Athletic Associations lobbies intensely against it. A secret group of over 300 colleges works the halls of Congress day and night in an attempt to stem the tide of Title IX. The core of this group is the College Football Association (CFA). CFA Director Edmund Joyce recently declared, "The specter of HEW regulations concerning Title IX...has the potential of being the most serious threat to intercollegiate football in its history."[2] Reverend Joyce is evidently referring to the widely held and completely incorrect notion that Title IX will require universities to spend the exact same amount of money on men's and women's programs. In light of the tremendous expenditures of the CFA's sixty members on football and basketball, that might present a problem.

"... unequal aggregate expenditure for members of each sex or unequal expenditures for male and female teams ... will not constitute non-compliance with this section ..."

TITLE IX Regulation

But Title IX does *not* require exactly equal spending and Reverend Joyce, the CFA, and the NCAA all know it. Title IX requires *substantially* equal per capita expenditures with the following exceptions: contact sports or sports which are contested nationally instead of regionally. What the CFA is really up to is cutting costs for college sports. At the 1979 NCAA convention they proposed that scholarships for all sports except men's football and basketball be eliminated. If the proposal had passed, it would have meant the end of all women's and "minor" sports, which are just an annoying nuisance to the CFA and the networks.

There are times, however, when the CFA members are willing to find a spot for women on their teams. The University of Alabama offers thirteen full scholarships to women who act as "athletic hostesses." Their job is to entice prospective recruits to sign up with the Crimson Tide.

"We'll comply the last minute of the last day."[3]

SUPERINTENDENT OF SCHOOLS;
Fairview, Arkansas

The struggle for equitable funding does not spring merely from the desires of a handful of militant women. A recent Harris Poll indicated that 93 percent of all parents want their sons *and daughters* to participate in physical fitness programs and sports. Yet today women receive only 14 percent of school athletic operating budgets although they pay more than half of all tuition and fees.

What's Wrong with This Picture?

Maybe as you've been reading this chapter you've gotten the funny feeling that something is missing. Like a band without a bass player or the puzzle books that ask "What's wrong with this picture?" Well, something is missing. The struggle for women's equality in sports has been almost exclusively limited to white, middle-class women. Almost all women professional athletes are in this category. This makes them ideal for product marketing in the burgeoning women's sports business. But it also means that women's professional sports have relied on the very tenuous "goodwill" of opportunist coporations like Bonne Bell, Avco, Colgate, Virginia Slims, etc. In August 1979 Colgate announced they would drop their sponsorship of several women's sports events at a savings of nearly $2 million.

"By reducing the level of our involvement in sports sponsorship, we are freeing up financial and management resources, which can be redirected toward growth opportunities elsewhere in the company."[4]
        KEITH CRANE, President, Colgate-Palmolive

College women are certainly entitled to equal participation in sports. But that shouldn't mean that everyone else gets left out in the cold. Most women never get to college. The high school dropout rate for Puerto Rican women is 75 percent; for Mexican-American women, 77 per cent; for Native American women, 90 percent; and the spiralling costs of education have not just affected minorities. Fewer than half the poor whites in the United States who have high academic ability will ever attend a single college class. The Bakke decision only reinforces these patterns.

Yvette Lewis is a basketball star at all-black Fremont High School in Los Angeles. The school is so poor that three different girls' teams have to share the same set of uniforms. If Yvette continues to excel and gets a scholarship and an education, everything is fine. But what good will Title IX be to her if she tears up her knee in a high school game?

"I do think black women are kinda left out in our society."[5]
        GINO VANELLI

They are certainly left out of the women's sports movement. This was clearly demonstrated by a 1979 issue of *Women's Sports* magazine. It carried a long article on a bunch of women who make money in various sports businesses. Anything on black women and their particular problems in sports? No. Puerto Rican women? No. Mexican women? No. Appalachian women? No. Filipino women? No. Indian women? No. I humbly submit that the problems these women face just trying to get some exercise are more important than those of women trying to make a million dollars selling jogging bras.

The Southern Belle Moves Northward

The special problems of the South and its effect on sports throughout the country are also generally ignored. In terms of girls' participation in high school sports, North Carolina ranks 41st; Mississippi, 42nd; Virginia, 45th; Arkansas, 46th; South Carolina, 47th; Louisiana, 48th; and Alabama, dead last.

Mississippi does not even have a compulsory education law. New corporations pay no taxes for the their first ten years of operation. Small wonder that Mississippi has one of the worst girls' athletic programs in the whole country. When the superintendent of schools in Starkville, Mississippi was asked how he planned to adjust his athletic budget to accomodate girls, he replied, "That's a good one. We don't have much of a budget anyway."[6]

The Taft-Hartley Act has allowed Southern states to pass right-to-work (open shop) laws. As a result, the South has the weakest unions and lowest wages in the country. This means less tax revenue and shabby or non-existent athletic programs. Coupled with the tax breaks corporations receive in the South, it is impossible to build the financial base necessary to support an adequate sports program. The creation of this southern industrial paradise has also meant that hundreds of companies have closed their northern plants and built new ones in the Sunbelt. This in turn has eroded the tax base of northern cities so severely that now *their* athletic programs have begun to fall by the wayside.

The South has also acted as a powerful political brake on the progress of women's sports. Twelve of the fifteen states which have not yet ratified the Equal Rights Amendment are southern right-to-work states. North Carolina is a good example. It is the seventh most industrialized state in the country; 61 percent of its workers are women. Yet it is the least unionized state and has the lowest industrial wages. North Carolina has defeated the ERA four straight times and North Carolina Senator Jesse Helms is a national leader of the anti-ERA movement.

There is a solid bloc of 124 southern congressmen, mostly from the plantation belt, who have never voted for any legislation that would benefit women. They are a reliable ally of the powerful foes of Title IX.

Jackie Onassis or Rosie the Riveter?

The women's sports movement has two paths open to it. It can continue to focus on the athletic and business success of a small group of women *or* it can shift its emphasis to the vast majority of women who are generally left out of American political life: women in the ghettos and the barrios; on the reservations and in the backwaters of the South, the Southwest, and Appalachia. Sports must be made available to the women who work in the fields from California to the Rio Grande Valley to Florida; to the women who labor in the textile mills of Georgia and the Carolinas; to the women who create our electronic hardware in the silicon valleys of California, Texas, and Massachusetts; and to the countless women who wait on tables, work in offices, or clean other people's homes.

The developing world economic crisis and subsequent militarization of the U.S. economy mean that in the future there will be even less money for sports offered up by the various levels of government. We can be sure we'll be told that women's sports programs can be funded only at the expense of men's. (Notre Dame eliminated men's hockey scholarships and gave the money to the women's athletic program.) Some women's groups have endorsed this approach.

However, it is just not true that there isn't enough money

for women *and* men. Each year we are presented with a smaller and smaller pie to divide up. If we continue to squabble over the size of the slices we will see the pie become a cupcake and than a cookie.

Only when men and women realize that they have no fundamental conflict of interest will we be able to take the fight we should be waging over the *size of the pie* to the bakery in Washington, D.C.

Recruit-Out on the Plantation: The Economics of College Sports

College sports are really just professional sports with lower wages.

Ohio State *nets* more than $400,000 from every home football game. Seventy schools divided more than $16 million from the proceeds of 1979 bowl games while the Rose, Orange and Cotton Bowls alone generate over $100 million for local businesses every New Year's Day. The NCAA will receive $118 million from ABC for television rights to football games for 1978-81. The gross earnings of the 1980 NCAA basketball tournament were $6.2 million.

"The main thing is keeping gate receipts as high as possible."[1]
    ARTHUR HANSEN, President of Purdue University

A coalition of over 300 schools has lobbied Congress intensely in an attempt to gut Title IX (equality of funding for women's sports). They claim that equality for women will destroy intercollegiate sports. But not one of those 300 schools will open their athletic financial records to the public. Are they afraid the alumni will see how well off they really are?

It is certainly true that some schools have been forced to make cutbacks due to financial problems. When the City College of New York began to charge tuition in 1979, more than 35,000 students were forced to leave. West Texas State has reduced scholarships and eliminated coaches. Georgia and UCLA have done away with wrestling. Colorado State, Utah,

Idaho, Southern Methodist, and several other schools have dropped baseball while the Atlantic Coast Conference has eliminated its indoor track championships.

However, the financial fortunes of a university and "its" athletic department seldom go hand in hand. One college lobbied the state legislature for funds to pay faculty salaries while the athletic department had a $2.3 million surplus. So the athletic department *lent* the university $400,000.

In the last ten years athletic costs have more than doubled, but TV revenues have increased even more rapidly. Most major schools have built new stadiums or arenas and they must be filled. Losing teams don't fill seats and they don't attract TV contracts either. Pressure mounts on coaches to win, not because Americans have some irrational need to be Number One but because there's so much money at stake.

Notre Dame is a good example. Its football team is on national television at least twice a year to the tune of $1 million. The 1978 Cotton Bowl brought in another million. It has its own worldwide football radio network, which encompasses 400 stations and brings in $400,000 a year. So it really has little to do with "building character" or "winning one for the Gipper." (George Gipp twice transferred from Notre Dame when offered more money by other schools.) The sports revenue is already in the budget and the coaches must come up with it.

Birth of a Salesman

In 1966 Ohio State's football team went from a 7-2 record the previous year to 4-5 and alumni contributions dropped by $500,000. In 1960 Missouri improved its record from 6-5 to 10-1 and alumni donations went up $175,000. Such idiocy puts a lot of pressure on coaches and it boils down to pressure to recruit.

"There have been a number of factors which have changed things off the court, most importantly recruiting. Recruiting these days is much more intense than it used to be. Seven or eight years ago, a head coach rarely went to court a prospect, the assistants took care of that. Today, though, you go watch

high school games several times a week rather than just going occasionally to watch a superstar like in the 60's. As a result the older coaches like myself have had to change a lot or get out."²

JOHN ORR, Iowa State basketball coach

Colleges have even legalized the pressure. San Diego State basketball coach Tim Vezie's contract specified that he had to win 15 games by February 12, 1979. He didn't and was fired.

Sometimes the recruiter is just a guy from the neighborhood like basketball "superscout" Rodney Parker of Brooklyn. But usually he's an assistant coach, a position which has been reduced to travelling salesman. He may be a great guy but he's in a bind. He wants a career as a head coach and there's nothing wrong with that. But he won't even be an assistant for long if he doesn't bring in the material for a winner. So what does he do if a kid asks him about the weather ("Well, Jim, it's a very dry type of cold.") or about whether there's any social life for blacks? He lies. What does he do if he is losing a hot prospect to another school that passes out $100 bills or finds jobs for the family? He cheats. This is not to condone the sick things that are often done in the recruiting wars. But under the present set-up there is too much money at stake for it to be any other way.

Politicians have been slow to create jobs for youth. But if a young man can handle a bat or ball, they will be on him quicker than flies on fertilizer. The West Virginia legislature declared Rod Thorn a state asset to pressure him into attending the University of West Virginia. The New Orleans City Council unsuccessfully tried to get local boy Rick Robey to sign with Tulane. Ted Kennedy, who has called for a crackdown by the courts on unemployed youth, often takes prospective Harvard athletes to lunch in the Senate dining room.

The parents sometimes get more attention than the son or daughter. But Adrian Dantley's mother found that things changed after her son signed with Notre Dame. She no longer received invitations from Hubert Humphrey or Governor Marvin Mandel. The mailbox was no longer filled with letters from the likes of Arnold Palmer and that congressman from North Carolina no longer cared if she was free for lunch.

Like everything else, recruiting costs money. A New Mexico assistant coach spent three months in a Petersburg, Virginia motel in a vain attempt to recruit Moses Malone. The University of Maryland *did* sign Moses after they spent $20,000 on the chase. That money could have helped to renovate a school in Baltimore's inner city. To recruit (and lose) Larry Miller, Duke spent $12,000, money that could have paid for a health and safety inspector for the textile mills of the Carolinas. The University of Oklahoma allows football coach Barry Switzer to spend $120,000 distributing videotapes of his TV show around the world. While it's comforting to know that people in Tokyo and guys working the North Sea oil rigs won't miss Barry's words of wisdom, wouldn't it make more sense to use that money to build a recreation complex for the Cherokee people of eastern Oklahoma?

The NCAA: Just Doing Their Job

Why doesn't the NCAA do more about recruiting abuses? Do they need a larger enforcement staff?

To understand why the NCAA does so little, its role and function must be better understood. In the words of former U.S. Senator Marlow Cook, the NCAA is "a body primarily designed to protect and defend its member institutions from the professional sports world and to make sure that collegiate sports gets its share of the sports business pie."[3] The NCAA knows very well what goes on in the dark corners of collegiate sports but they step in only if abuses threaten to raise the costs of the members.

In fact, the only reason the NCAA has any enforcement staff at all is to keep recruiting costs in line. Consider the alternative. What if Walter Byers, chairman of the board of the NCAA, came right out and said, "OK, guys, we all know we're in the business of buying athletes and all this pretend stuff is getting to be a real pain in the ass, so just go out and do it." High school stars would get agents. They would more effectively pit one school against another and their "salaries" would increase dramatically. To avoid such a disaster, the schools put up with the NCAA and its occasional meddling. In return, the NCAA does everything it can to help keep costs down. It lobbies against equal funding for women. It passed a rule which makes a transferring athlete (but not a coach who breaks his contract) ineligible for a year. Without that rule, the bidding war for transfers would get too costly.

"All universities conspire to hold down athletes' wages. The formal name of this conspiracy is the National Collegiate Athletic Association. The NCAA is so devoted to the principle of amateurism that it doesn't want athletes to sully themselves by making real money from the NCAA members' multi-million dollar athletic program."[4]

GEORGE WILL, *syndicated columnist*

But the NCAA has taste and discretion. It doesn't penalize just anybody. Ohio State has more alumni than any other school, which makes it a prime television team. It never gets penalized. Notre Dame has tremendous worldwide popularity and it brings in *beaucoups* TV dollars. Absolutely untouchable. Walter Byers asks us to believe that the Ohio States, Notre Dames, and Alabamas never recruit illegally. Only schools like Southwestern Louisiana or Long Beach State.

What about Oklahoma? Yes, they have been penalized severely and there are three reasons. 1) The Sooners' recruiting budget is out of hand, even for a Top Ten team, and the other powers use the NCAA to try to force Oklahoma to play by the rules of the cartel. 2) Oklahoma alumni have less national influence than those of many other majors. 3) The NCAA has to pick on one of the big boys from time to time to maintain public credibility. But the NCAA whistle-blowers have been known to give the Sooners a make-up call. In 1977 Darrell Shepard was one of the most sought-after prep quarterbacks in the country. He signed with Houston but was ruled ineligible for all post-season games because he allegedly was given a sports car. The NCAA declared that he could play in bowl games *if* he left the Southwest Conference. In 1979 Darrell Shepard became a student at Oklahoma. Walter Byers was *so* surprised.

"The sooner universities understand that college athletics is big business, and they need businessmen running it, the better off they'll be."[5]

TOBY WARREN, athletic director,
Southwestern Louisiana

Somebody is listening, Toby. Don Canham of Michigan is a millionaire businessman. Southern Methodist has a stockbroker as athletic director and in 1977 Princeton hired Robert Myslik, a chemical company comptroller.

When penalties do come down, they are not against the alumni or the athletic directors. These fine gentlemen keep right on living the good life. Larry Gillard never had the good life, which was why he needed the scholarship to Mississippi State in the first place. But the NCAA took his scholarship away and declared him permanently ineligible because he accepted a $12.50 discount at a local clothing store. The discount was offered to all students but that didn't faze the NCAA. The same organization that spent $1.4 million just for public relations in 1977 took away Larry Gillard's chance at an athletic career because of a $12.50 discount. It took away Oklahoma State football player Mike Edward's eligibility because he accepted a ten-mile car ride from an assistant coach while in high school. When Minnesota basketball player David Winey received a 75-cent Jolly Green Giant tote bag, he found himself charged with "accepting an illegal gift."

An athlete charged by the NCAA is presumed guilty and in reality not even allowed to defend himself. When Mike Edwards appealed his sentence, the hearing was held more than a thousand miles from the school. He could not afford the plane fare, and the NCAA refused to let his lawyers pay it. When the NCAA issues an OI (letter of Official Inquiry) to a school, this is supposed to *start* the investigation. But not once in the history of the NCAA has an accused party received an OI and then been acquitted. A coach or athlete brought up on charges cannot confront his accuser or bring witnesses to the proceedings. The investigators are not required to produce documented evidence. If there is an appeal, the accused is not allowed to have a copy of the transcript of the original hearing.

"A lot of rules are unrealistic, especially for the poor black kids. A lot of times I wonder, where does the ghetto black athlete even get a suitcase to go anywhere? What do you do when a kid needs a pair of pants? What do you do when a kid's mother is sick, 1500 miles away, and he's at your school only because he plays basketball? How does he get home?"[6]

AL McGUIRE

Long Hours, Low Pay

The basic premise of the economic relationships in college sport—that the athletes do all the work and the schools, networks, and advertisers get all the money—is wrong. Three year ago basketball ticket sales at Michigan State amounted to $150,000. In 1979, Magic Johnson's sophomore year, the total was $425,000. Add to that the tournament money, $25,000 for a TV game with Kansas, and even increased football revenues which were attributed to the drawing power of Magic Johnson. In return he probably got a few thousand dollars, maybe a car and an apartment.

"Now when I get a kid to play in that stadium, I know the kid's going to bring us in $50,000 or $60,000 a year. Now what in the hell is he going to get in return?"[7]

WOODY HAYES

People don't realize how hard college athletes work. Football requires up to four hours of practice a day, often done while the player is in pain from an injury. Following the last game of the season, the players plunge into an off-season conditioning program voluntary in name only. Then come five weeks of spring practice followed by a detailed summer workout schedule. After that there's pre-season summer practice in intense heat while the other students are still at the beach. These guys deserve every penny they don't get.

> *"... The fans around here are something. They come into Norman for a game, drink their beer, their wine, have a good time. They don't put in all the work, suffer all the pain. You hear them: 'Oh, I can't wait for football! I just can't wait!' Well, I can wait. I can wait. I'm in no hurry to get back out there and sweat and have to whirlpool my body so it don't hurt so much. Oh, no, I can wait."[8]*
>
> *BILLY SIMS, Heisman Trophy winner, 1979*

Recent limitations on the number of scholarships a school can offer have made the position of the non-superstar still more tenuous. These limitations were not imposed to "curb recruiting abuses" or to "put sports in their proper perspective." It was simply a matter of reducing costs. That means cutting athletes. For example, in football a school can award 30 new scholarships each year but can only carry a total of 95. Since four classes, freshman through senior, at 30 scholarships each comes to 120, simple arithmetic shows that 25 guys have got to go.

That is a problem for coaches, since it is illegal to revoke a scholarship just because a player hasn't lived up to expectations. But there are ways to deal with the player who refuses to sign away his scholarship voluntarily. Tutors are suddenly too busy to help; maybe the kid will flunk out. At some schools, special squads are formed of players who won't give up their scholarships. They are put through hour after hour of meaningless drills until they see the light. Anything goes to open up another spot for a high school senior who may do a better job.

Freshman eligibility is another cost-cutter. It eliminates the need to recruit an entire team of freshmen and an extra year of profits can be squeezed out of those who can play right away.

"I Was Just Following Orders"

The profitability of winning forces coaches to uphold many of the seamier traditions of college sports. A coach just cannot afford to let a good athlete flunk out, and I mean that literally. As Woody Hayes said, "We have an investment in each kid, and if he's a flunk-out, we've lost our money."[9] Our educational system often presents coaches with high school graduates who can't even read, so they fill up the athlete's schedules with Volleyball 122 or Weightlifting 206 in a desperate struggle to keep them eligible. Individual coaches cannot change this situation. The university would not support any effort to give the athletes a real education. The revelations that athletes at New Mexico, USC, and other schools were given credit for courses they never attended should come as no surprise. Any administrator who claims he doesn't know these practices are commonplace is either lying or not doing his job. You win 15 games by February 12 or you're gone.

Why do coaches put up with all this? Well, if they play their cards right and figure out how to make some corporation a pile of money, their share can be considerable. Equipment manufacturers are always happy to place an envelope on the coach's desk to help him make those difficult decisions. But the master is probably University of Iowa football coach Hayden Fry. Though the years he has acquired oil and gas wells, racehorses, and sports camps. But in 1980 he went for the brass ring. He, or rather his advertising agency, developed a line of 50 different Fry-Hawk souvenirs (such as a beer mug emblazoned with his rugged features) and sold the rights to J.C. Penney.

Pressure to win accounts for the almost universal practice of forcing athletes to play hurt. While any coach who does it should be fired on the spot, his successor will be hard put to avoid doing the same thing. Charley Taylor, former All-Pro with the Washington Redskins, tells the following story: "In spring training my sophomore year, I broke my neck—four vertebrae. 'Hey, Coach,' I said, 'my neck don't feel good.' 'There's nothing wrong with your neck, you jackass,' he said. So the numb went away a little, and I made a tackle. When I went to get up, my body got up but my head just stayed there, on the ground. The coach says, 'Hey, get this jackass off the field.' So the trainer puts some ice on my neck and after practice they took me up to the infirmary for an x-ray. The doctor said, 'Son, your neck is broken. You got here ten minutes later, you'd be dead.' Dead! Man, that scared me. I mean those colleges let you lie right out there on the field and die. That's something to think about."[10]

If, during all this, a player jumps to the pros, *he* is called ungrateful. If an athlete suffers a permanent injury which prevents him from playing pro ball, will the grateful college pay him his share of the money he made for them so he can get a new start in life? Of course not.

One Way Out

Why don't the athletes do something about the situation? Their position is weak because they have so few alternatives. The national youth unemployment rate is 20 percent and over 45 percent for minorities. College athletes are well represented among the 39 million Americans the AFL-CIO has estimated to be functionally illiterate. The schools of the United States are rapidly going bankrupt; this hits national minorities the hardest. (In New York City there is one teacher for every 8 white students; one for every 84 blacks; one for every 262 Puerto Ricans). The reinstitution of the draft is imminent and movies like *The Deer Hunter* and *The Boys in Company C* show the youth what their fate may well be. In other words, many of the young people in this country don't have much of a future and they know it. Is it any wonder that they grasp at any straw they can?

If you point out to a senior varsity high school athlete that the odds against his playing even one minute in the pros are 20,000-1, he may well reply that that's better than no chance at all. When the coach tells him to get a pain-killing shot and play on a broken ankle, does he really have a choice? He may get crippled for life, but there's also a slim chance he may get to the pros and be able to support a family.

A Final Note

Of the 2,191 tickets allotted to the University of North Carolina for the 1979 ACC post-season basketball tournament, students were allowed to buy 100. All others were sold to people who had donated at least $8,100 to the athletic scholarship fund. That's right, and at $8,100 for a four-session ticket, that's $50.63 per minute of Tar Heel basketball. That's where it's at in college sports today.

Rules Are All Right If There's Someone Left to Play the Game: The Economics of High School Sports

Twenty percent of all school districts in the United States—and this includes some of the wealthiest—have either reduced or eliminated their athletic programs. California's athletic programs have been decimated by Proposition 13. Cleveland has eliminated all junior high sports. Oakland has closed all of its neighborhood public playgrounds. New York City has eliminated after-school gym programs. Schools in Michigan, Illinois, Indiana, and Idaho have eliminated football. A few years ago it was nationwide news when a major school system had to close for even a few days. Today extended shutdowns are so common that new ones scarcely cause a raised eyebrow. The winter closing of the Toledo school system has become an annual event; the Chicago school system teeters on the brink of oblivion.

"We had too much community support, too many of our boys and girls were involved, the tradition of athletics in our school system was too long to think our Board of Education would ever consider axing the entire program. Yes, we would have to tighten our belts, but lose our programs, NEVER! We all believed that a complete loss of program just couldn't happen to us."[1]

DR. GEORGE ASCHENBRENNER, Assistant School Superintendent, Rockford, Illinois

---

Are you saying to yourself, "It can't happen here"? Don't count on it.

Obviously, when the schools are closed there is no sports program.

Today, teachers are forced to strike to protect themselves from the ravages of inflation and to try to improve the quality of education. Such was the case in a bitter six-week strike in Boardman, Ohio, in the fall of 1980. The strike also caused the cancellation of five football games which meant a loss of 30 percent of the entire athletic budget. No teachers, no sports.

Three referees' associations in southeastern Wisconsin threatened a one-day boycott of all games to protest the fact that their fee, in real dollars, is only 53 percent of what it was ten years ago. No refs, no sports.

Even where sports programs continue, the problems are enormous. Rising costs and budget cuts have forced many schools to raise their ticket prices; this has often led to a decline in attendance and revenues. Night crime and vandalism have meant that some schools schedule football and even basketball games in the afternoon; this also usually results in lower attendance.

An increase in injuries coupled with the greed of insurance companies have caused the cost of premiums to skyrocket. Insurance costs alone threaten to put many school districts out of the sports business. Some districts have seen a year-to-year increase in premiums of up to *600 percent!* Many "minor" sports have been axed due to insurance costs, and football and basketball may be next. Our schools are being held for ransom. In one California district the board was told that liability insurance would be renewed only if the board *eliminated all athletic and physical education programs.* John Klumb, director of physical education for the state of California, said, "It's at a point where, if we don't get some relief, the insurance companies will be allowed to dictate our curriculum to us."[2]

In the fall of 1979, more than 1000 New York City coaches stayed off the job for four weeks to force the city to restore a 25 percent pay cut they had voluntarily taken four years earlier but which was supposed to have been restored within two years. The coaches were supported by thousands of students of all nationalities and from all boroughs. They staged walkouts, boycotts, and marches. Finally, Mayor Koch promised to raise the money from private sources. Perhaps due to a guilty conscience, New York City realtors threw a few thousand dollars into the pot. They are largely responsible for the schools' financial woes in the first place, since they have refused to pay over $500 million in back real estate taxes.

Cities such as Detroit, Buffalo, and Philadelphia have been able to keep high school sports going only through donations from business and/or grassroots fund drives. The problems with this approach can be seen in Rock Island, Illinois, where the chairman of a private fund-raising drive wound up as president of the school board. Dick Fischer, who ran the Save Our Sports fund drive in Buffalo, said, "I don't feel the sports program should be funded this way. I wouldn't want to do it again."[3] The obvious question is: "Where will you get the money next year?"

Some schools are getting it from the kids. Several California schools now charge each student money for every sport he or she participates in.

High Finance, Low Blows

Where does the money go, anyway? Books, salaries, school maintenance and construction? Gyms, coaches, uniforms? Well, yes. But as much as 30 percent goes to pay for the interest on school bonds. When the school board comes to you every spring to vote for a new levy, it's not for books or shoulder pads. It's to pay the banks the interest on previous loans. The American worker already labors from January to May to pay taxes. School levies fare badly at the polls because it just doesn't seem right that the local government needs even more of our money. Without those bank interest payments, there would be no need for school levies.

The collapse of the bond market in early 1980 has made fund-raising for schools next to impossible. Cities and states which had hoped to float bond issues and pay only six or seven percent interest on them have found that there are often no takers until the rate is hiked to nine percent or more. Few municipalities can afford such a deal. In Ypsilanti, Michigan, plans for a new school had to be shelved when there were no buyers at eight percent.

"In Oregon, the state found no takers recently for more than $50 million in bonds. Proceeds would have financed housing for the elderly and school buildings. The bonds had an eight percent interest ceiling and Wall Street simply demanded more."[4]
                    THE WALL STREET JOURNAL

A student in Toledo summed up the situation when she said, "Football season has been cancelled due to too much interest."

School Funding, Then and Now

How did we get in such a mess? To understand, we need to take a brief look at the history of school funding. Unlike collegiate sports, where the athletic department generally stands apart from the university it supposedly represents, and in some cases is even legally separate, high school athletic and academic finances go hand-in-hand. A high school athletic department cannot exist without a financially viable school system, whereas the major college athletic powers could probably function independently even if their respective universities went bankrupt.

Maestro, a little history please:

Education in the United States in the nineteenth century was decentralized and generally tied to religious institutions. Its basic aim was to give children enough of the three R's to enable them to work in the rapidly growing industries of the North.

The proportion of five- to seventeen-year-olds in school rose from 57 percent in 1860 to 80 percent in 1920. As the cities grew, the one-room schoolhouse began to disappear. The large numbers of schoolchildren forced the government to raise money through taxation. But this was generally inadequate. The difference was often made up by donations from wealthy families. It was during this period that school funding became tied to the local tax base.

During the Depression the federal government was forced to allocate massive funds to prevent the total collapse of public education. The funding role of state governments increased as local tax bases were depressed by the movement of factories out of cities.

Since World War II the local share of school expenditures has fallen from 61 percent to 48 percent while state and federal shares have risen proportionately. In the last ten years two new developments have virtually exploded on the scene and threaten to destroy our traditional ability to fund a school system for the majority of the people.

The Electronics Revolution

The impact of computers on employment has been tremendous. Today the information industry employs 53 percent of the total U.S. work force. The computer has already conquered the fields of communications and accounting, and manufacturing is next. For example, at the Ford steering gear plant in Indianapolis, rack and pinion assemblies are virtually untouched by human hands. The assemblies are loaded and unloaded by people, but are assembled, inspected, and tested electronically under the control of a computer. And we ain't seen nothin' yet. The computer and the factory have announced their engagement but the marriage has yet to be consummated. The rest of this century will see an incredible electronic revolution in industry. General Electric has plans to replace 18,000 assembly line workers with robots while General Motors will triple its in-plant robot population by 1983.

These developments create a demand for a relatively small number of engineers and programmers and at the same time tend to eliminate the need for skilled industrial labor. The economy no longer requires a large, skilled, blue collar workforce. The percentage of workers with a high school diploma fell from 79 percent in 1959 to 62 percent in 1979.

This means more and better technical education for the few, worse education for the many. How else can you explain the emergence of tens of millions of functionally illiterate adults in the United States? Why can't 25 percent of our seventeen-year-olds do a simple multiplication problem?

As our school systems slowly erode to conform to the needs

of industry, it is the so-called "frills" that are cut back first. In some cities music is the first to go but usually it is sports: varsity, intramural, physical education. "The tradition of athletics in our school system was too long to think our Board would ever consider axing the entire program . . ."

The electronics revolution should mean boundless opportunities for recreation by freeing mankind from backbreaking toil. The silicon chip should mean a 20-hour work week for everyone. Instead, it means zero hours for one section of the population and overtime for most of the rest. Automation in the factories, printing plants, and offices means there are fewer workers to pay taxes. Fewer tax dollars make further cuts in school athletic budgets inevitable.

Southbound

In the last twenty years the cities of the North and West have seen factories close up shop and leave town at an ever-increasing pace. Akron, Ohio was once the rubber capital of the world; today it is an industrial ghost town. Chicago lost 200,000 manufacturing jobs between 1968 and 1976. In the decade between 1966 and 1976, Massachusetts lost 103,100 jobs—14 percent of the state's total. In the same period New York City lost 600,000 jobs. It doesn't take Sherlock Holmes to find out where these jobs have gone. They have been relocated largely in the South and Southwest, where wages are lower and unions weaker due to right-to-work laws, and where corporate tax rates are low or nonexistent. Many northern states have responded by further lowering their corporate taxes in a futile attempt to hold industry. The result has been that even less money is available for schools and their athletic programs.

The flight of industry to the South has not meant any relative improvement in opportunity for Southern athletes. The South is not rising to the level of the North. Slowly but surely, *the entire country is being dragged down to the level of the South.*

What does the "level of the South" mean in terms of high school sports? It means the lowest level of participation for *all* sports, including football. It means the lowest level of participation and funding for girls' athletics. This is what the North and West can look forward to if present trends remain unchecked.

The leaders of Northern cities and states have frantically limboed to the suicidal beat of "How low can you go?" as they cut business taxes and slash essential social services in a vain attempt to get their corporate lovers to stay home. This has not and will not work and soon the Northern athlete will have to try to make do with an athletic infrastructure that resembles that of Mississippi or Mexico.

But we don't have to just sit and cry in our Lite Beer about it. What can we do? Turn the page and read on.

Sports in the South:
A Different Ballgame

It crops up everywhere. The songs of the Charlie Daniels Band. The movie *Easy Rider*. White lightnin' and revenooers. Southern-style cooking. The Southern strategy. To Northerners and Southerners alike, the South is different. Sports are no exception. It is not just that certain sports, like stock car racing, are much more popular south of the Mason-Dixon line. Participation in sports is lower in the South than in any other region despite the fact that the South has undergone tremendous industrial growth in the past 25 years and enjoys the best weather in the country. The low participation is true of every state and every sport with very few exceptions (Texas for boys' high school volleyball; Arkansas for boys' high school tennis). Per capita participation in all high school sports (see Appendix II) is 3 percent lower than the national average in Texas, 28 percent lower in Virginia and Tennessee, 30 percent lower in South Carolina, 48 percent lower in Florida, 49 percent lower in Mississippi, 50 percent lower in Louisiana, and 56 percent lower in North Carolina, the country's least unionized state. The only exceptions are Georgia, which hovers around the national average, and Arkansas, which is considerably above it.

A brief look at education in the South shows why this low rate of participation is inevitable. Southern schools spend an average of $1,076 per pupil versus a national average of $1,388. Teachers' and coaches' salaries average $12,070 nationally but only $9,136 in the South. A school superintendent in South Carolina fixes the school buildings with his own hands, since there is no money for maintenance in the school budget. In Noxubee County, Mississippi, teachers wait in vain for the arrival of requisitioned sports equipment. In Maxton, North Carolina, the school buildings are on the verge of falling down but no money is forthcoming to renovate them.

This isn't happening because the South is still a relatively rural area. All other rural regions in the United States have *above-average* participation in sports. It is happening because low corporate taxes result in fewer high school boys playing football in the South than anywhere else in the country. Lower wages in the South also reduce the tax base. In 1975 the average Southern worker made $1.80 an hour less than his or her Northern counterpart. By 1979 that gap had widened to $2.50 an hour. The historically developed color hatred has resulted in the consistent reduction of sports opportunities for blacks and whites. Throughout the South there are public school systems which are all black and have little money for books and salaries, let alone sports. For example, the Plains, Georgia School Board sits on a $200,000 surplus it refuses to spend to improve the public schools, which are 75 percent black. In these same areas the white children go to private academies, often paid for with public funds. While these private academies are generally better-equipped and financed (usually by local businessmen), the poor quality of their athletic programs would cause open rebellion in Ohio or California.

What about the "New South"? Certainly there have been changes in the South. Atlanta, Birmingham, Charlotte, New Orleans, Houston, and Mobile have all become industrial centers—meccas of the runaway shop and the multinational corporation. In these cities Jim Crow more often works the alleys by night instead of marching down the boulevard in the noonday sun. A small but distinct group of blacks have been allowed to "make it" in the South. Over half the black elected officials in the United States are in the South, including 63 percent of the black mayors. So perhaps, in a certain sense, there is a new South. But the heart of the South—the former plantation area that stretches from Texas to Virginia and is known as the Black Belt—has not changed at all. Here the per capita income for both blacks and whites is only one-half what it is in the major Southern cities. There are vast differences between Atlanta and Wrightsville, Georgia; between Birmingham and Lowndes County, Alabama; between Memphis, Tennessee and Tchula, Mississippi.

Tchula is a town of 1500 people located in the heart of the Mississippi Delta. It is 80 percent black. Rundown shacks are the typical housing. There is only one industry in the town, a small textile plant owned by Pennsylvania businessmen. Strict segregation is maintained on every level. Although four of the five members of the Board of Aldermen are black, two of the blacks vote with the sole white to block any move toward progress. Five white families dominate the local economy.

Tchula is in Holmes County, one of the ten poorest in the entire country. In nearby Lexington, the county seat, the "colored" and "white" signs are still up in the doctors' offices. The county hospital has one wing for blacks, another for whites. Although 68 percent of the people in Holmes County are black, the public schools are 99.9 percent black. Almost all of the white students attend one of the three private white academies in the county.

In 1970 the annual per capita income in Holmes County was $1,916. For blacks it was $632 ($12.15 a week). Over 75 percent of the entire population does not have a high school education, since there are no jobs that require one. There is only one weak union local in the county although there are 23 factories. Forty-five percent of the people in Holmes County are on welfare. Under such conditions, it doesn't take a Howard Cosell to describe the athletic facilities. In Tchula they total one small red clay field with a hoop on a pole (no backboard).

The contrast between the Black Belt and Southern urban centers shows up again when we look at which produces the most college football players. While almost all rural Black Belt counties produce way below the national average, Memphis, Nashville, Knoxville, Jacksonville, and Fort Lauderdale all boast above-average production.

Hattiesburg, Mississippi turns out college players at four times the national average. Biloxi, Natchez, Atlanta, Miami, and Waycross, Georgia all do well but it's a different story in Eastabuchie, Mississippi.

The position of blacks in the South cannot help but be reflected in the inner cities of the North. The five boroughs of New York City supply only 13 percent of the national average of college football players although the suburban counties which surround New York City are able to maintain typical output. Detroit, Boston, St. Louis, San Francisco, Baltimore, Kansas City, Philadelphia, and Milwaukee struggle along at less than 60 percent of the national average.

While the average Southerner always finishes last in the sports participation race, the South has a wide network of resort complexes for the wealthy. Since 1960, the South has led the country in golf course construction and produces 37 percent of all touring professional golfers. Yet, in a pattern familiar in other resort areas such as the Bahamas and Jamaica, Southern states average only 75 percent of the national average participation in high school golf. South Carolina, home of Hilton Head, lags behind at less than half the U.S. norm.

Each spring the major league owners tune up their profit-making machines at spring training in Florida. Yet Florida ranks thirty-ninth nationally in the number of boys who play high school baseball.

The rural Black Belt is a heavy anchor that keeps the ship of ordinary men and women throughout the United States from getting underway to its destination of adequate sports and recreation for all. The position of blacks in the rural South holds down that of the rural whites. This in turn holds down the urban, industrial South. Birmingham's black per capita income was $1,502 in 1970 while per capita income in the city as a whole averaged $2,848. The national average was nearly $8,000. Collectively, the position of blacks and whites in the South holds down the rest of the country and it is worth noting that Southern whites earn $2,000 a year less than Northern blacks. Like the links in an anchor chain, each is definitely above the other but all are underwater and going nowhere fast.

The Way Out

There are a lot of rules in sports: infield fly rule, three seconds, intentional grounding, high-sticking. But everything in sports has been subordinated to one iron law that no player, owner, coach, or fan can violate: the need for business to make a maximum profit.

School sports budgets have been devastated by the loss of revenue due to plant closings, runaway shops, and the militarization of the economy. School districts are increasingly unable to offer a high enough interest rate on school bonds to attract investment from the coupon-clippers who control our destiny. In response, 3,000 booster clubs were forced to form the Booster Clubs of America (BCA). In a desperate attempt to keep their school athletic programs afloat, BCA made a deal with New Worlds of Fundraising, Inc. ("Your Partner in Profitability"). The BCA members sell New Worlds' mail order catalogue for $5 and get to keep $2.50 plus 2 percent of all catalogue sales. New Worlds, of course, gets 98 percent.

In other words, we are allowed to participate in or watch sports only to the degree that our need for recreation does not conflict with the decisions of banks and corporations. Ford Motor Company has shown us what happens when our desire to play ball conflicts with the Wall Street version of the "national interest." In June 1980, Ford did away with their Punt, Pass and Kick program. They preferred to take the money and invest it in their assembly plants in Argentina and South Africa. We can rest assured that those who must search frantically for a maximum return will not buy bonds to fund our school athletic programs or uniforms for the local Little League.

We have allowed a situation to develop where without corporate investment we cannot have sports. If this continues, our school systems will have to keep cutting programs and in some cases will close down altogether. Our youth leagues, built with such hard work and devotion by millions of people, will wither away. YMCAs will cut back on their programs, continue to raise membership fees to compensate for the unemployed who can no longer afford to belong, and then close. The thousands of industrial leagues, track clubs, and weightlifting clubs—which already live a hand-to-mouth existence—will die. "Minor" sports will fade from memory.

We cannot allow this to happen. The only way out is to change the rules of the game. We must discard the idea that we prosper only when the multinationals prosper, that our health and happiness must be dependent on their bottom line. There is no reason for anyone to be deprived of sport and recreation in a world of unlimited electronically directed productivity. We must put an end to car washes, bake sales, and Booster Clubs of Americas as a basis of sports financing.

"We girls need more uniforms (the boys have different uniforms for each sport) but we were told there wasn't enough money to equalize girls' uniforms. So we tried to help financially. Last year the girls had a bake sale and this year we sold light bulbs."[1]

WOMAN COACH, *Jefferson Parish, Louisiana*

But before we go onto the field to slug it out with the multinationals, we had better take a look at our team. We have tremendous talent, good speed, and incredible depth. But we are hampered by widespread internal dissension and the lack of a game plan. As long as we blame our problems on members of our own team—be they minorities, women, or foreign workers—there is no point in going onto the field. We're beaten before the kickoff.

We must realize that the solutions to problems in sports lie away from the playing field. With that in mind, let's outline the essential plays we need to execute to carry out our game plan.

Choosing a Team

Our varsity must be drawn mainly from labor which is still the majority of the U.S. population. There have been a few billion words written on the significance of working people in human history. I would like to summarize them with just one example: There were nationwide student strikes on more than one occasion to protest the Vietnam War. Yet these actions did little to affect the course of that war. However, it was obvious to most people on both sides of the question that if even a section of the workers in the United States had waged a sustained strike against the war, it would not have lasted very long.

A Southern Strategy

The focus must be on the South if we are to put an end to discrimination and to build the strength necessary to successfully take on the multinationals and break loose the funds we need for sports and recreation.

At present, the South is the Achilles heel of the American body politic. The second-class athletic programs in the South have always limited the level of such programs in the North. Thus, our game plan must be to end the status of the South as a virtual colony of Northern financial interests.

It can be done. During the Civil War, Northern white workers flocked into the Union Army in order to destroy slavery. Union locals turned themselves into militia units for the same purpose. They did so not on moral grounds, but because they clearly understood that they themselves were being reduced to slaves by the situation in the South. They were constantly reminded that if they did not accept wage cuts they would be replaced by slaves. Is it really that different today? In the spring of 1980 Dayton Press, Inc. told its 2,500 employees that they would have to accept a *15-year wage freeze* or the company would shift its operations to the South.

Any effort not conducted on the scale of the Civil War is doomed to failure. First and foremost, the South must be organized. Labor must focus its vast human and financial resources on this campaign. Then and only then can the destructive competition between regions be ended. Only then can the iron grip of Southern politicians over the entire country be broken.

The first opponent on the schedule for organizing the South is the Taft-Hartley Act. To eliminate Taft-Hartley will require a massive campaign of organization and education. It means not being afraid to follow the example of the United Mine Workers who openly defied Taft-Hartley and the President of the United States during the 1978 coal strike.

The Backstabbers

Our game plan will not be complete until we realize that two key players on the multinationals' team are the government and the majority of top international union officials.

For example, after World War II the federal government spent over $15 billion to help corporations move to the South. The excuse given was that it was necessary to fulfill production goals for the Marshall Plan. In reality, it was a conscious move to blunt the growing strength of organized labor and insure superprofits for the emerging multinationals.

The unorganized and confused state of the labor movement is not an accident. The labor movement is where it is today because certain people led it there. Rather than leading a drive to organize the South and Puerto Rico, these men are, in the wake of Reagan's election, trying to put together a team that can drive down the field for a rebuilt Democratic Party. They must be stopped at the line of scrimmage if we are ever going to get our hands on the ball.

Brother, Can You Spare A Dime?

The funds already exist to pay for a tremendous expansion of athletic and recreational facilities throughout the United States. Such a transformation can be paid for by taking money from the military budget and by thorough, *national* tax reform. Organizing the South will give us the power to make these proposals a reality.

- For every $1 billion spent on military projects, 45,000 jobs are created. For every $1 billion spent on public service jobs such as the construction of gymnasiums, 132,000 jobs are created.

- The *official* military budget is $161 billion. This does not include foreign military aid. Nor does it include billions in subsidies to the nuclear power industry, whose main function is to produce plutonium for nuclear weapons.

- Military spending is centered in the South and Southwest. Since the Korean War, 12 of the top 16 states in the military spending parade have been right-to-work states. From 1955 to 1975 the share of total military spending rose from 32 to 43 percent in the South and Southwest while it fell from 34 to 17 percent in the Northeast and Midwest. From 1970 to 1974 right-to-work states gained 547,000 military-connected jobs, but at a cost of 1,450,000 jobs in other states. U.S. workers pay nearly 60 percent of their taxes to create jobs in right-to-work states. We finance our own unemployment and the subsequent elimination of our athletic programs.

- From 1950 to 1976 corporate taxes rose from $10.8 billion to $46.7 billion, but individual taxes rose from $17 billion to $159 billion.

- There are 520,000 millionaires in the United States, 250 of whom paid no taxes in 1978.

- Many corporations simply refuse to pay their taxes and government efforts at collection can at best be described as feeble. The total outstanding in New York City and Chicago alone is over $1 billion.

"Houses are falling down. People are out of work. But this is our society. I haven't been able to understand giving all this money for defense."[2]
        LARRY BROWN, 1970 NFL rushing leader

Do you want to see $30 billion of your money spent on the MX missile or on recreation and education? Do you want your kids to go to war or to the Y?

When the Going Gets Tough, the Tough Get Going

Obviously, the problems we face will not be easy to solve. It is a complicated and difficult battle and will become more so in the future. All I can say is, jump in. The water isn't fine but it's the only way to get to the other side.

Questionnaire

What do you think are the biggest problems in sports today?

- ☐ Corporate control of sports
- ☐ Discrimination against minorities
- ☐ Player salaries
- ☐ Lack of funding
- ☐ Discrimination against women
- ☐ Fan/Player Violence
- ☐ Athlete Exploitation by Colleges
- ☐ Lack of opportunity for youth
- ☐ Politics and sports
- ☐ Other
  Please specify _____

Comments:

Did you favor a boycott of the 1980 Olympics by the United States?

☐ Yes   ☐ No
Why or why not?

_____
Name

_____
Address

_____
City   State   Zip

Send to: All-Star Features
          Box 1041
          Warren, Ohio 44481

Appendix I

The following is a column by John Schulian from the *Chicago Sun-Times* (April 23, 1979). It is reprinted by permission of Mr. Schulian and the *Sun-Times*.

This one is personal. It is about the striking major league umpires and the scabs who have replaced them and the trouble I have had trying to write about baseball's most shameful season. Blasting away shouldn't be a problem, of course. The issues in the strike are easily defined and the space in the paper is always there, but still I hesitate. Let me take a deep breath and I will tell you why. It is because I was a scab once.

I wish I could rid myself of the memory, cut it out and put it in a metal box and drop the box in the middle of Lake Michigan. But there is no way. I am stuck with it, just as the white-collar jocksniffers who have crossed picket lines to umpire this year will one day be stuck with theirs.

What they are doing, though they may not realize it now, is cowardly, illogical and contemptible. They are stealing from baseball's poor and giving it to its rich. They have come to the aid of the vilest men in the game—Comr. Bowie Kuhn, both league presidents and the team owners—men desperate to break the regular umpires so they can serve warning on the rebellious players' unions.

May the scabs who serve them so loyally have the same bad dreams I have.

The nightmare I can't get rid of began Oct. 1, 1975, one month to the day after I hitched my star to the *Washington Post*. I had endured five years of serfdom in Baltimore and now I was eager to sample the fame and fat paychecks that the *Post*, the paper that felled Richard Nixon, could offer. In one long, cold night, however, my new world was turned upside down as the *Post's* contract with the pressmen's union expired and the pressmen themselves exploded.

A foreman was badly beaten, all nine of the paper's presses were knocked out of commission, and the *Post* suffered the greatest indignity in the business—it was unable to publish for one full day. While my fellow newsroom liberals and I shook our heads in dismay, the upshot of the carnage slowly dawned on us: Our bluff was about to be called.

We were card-carrying members of the Newspaper Guild, a union composed largely of reporters and editors who think their college educations make them too good for any such thing. Only after much hesitation did many of us admit that The Guild, not our overwhelming intellect, was the reason we weren't still getting paid $125 a week. And so, like it or not, we were ready to honor picket lines set up in peace—our idea being that if we were ever driven to picketing, the courtesy would be returned.

But this business with the pressmen was different. It was violent and frightening and disorienting.

We retreated to the proud old church around the corner from the *Post* building and tried to make sense of what had happened. Some Guild members begged us to acknowledge the difference between a good strike and a bad one, just as we had acknowledged the difference between a good war and a bad one during the Vietnam era. Others argued that the pressmen's union was on the verge of being broken by management and that this was when our solidarity with our fellow laborers should be strongest, no matter how badly they strayed. The debate droned on for hours and hours and, finally, there was nothing left to do but settle our differences by voting.

We voted once, twice, thrice, as I recall, and we voted on three different days. Each time, I voted against crossing the picket line. I want you to know that. It is the one thing I have to be proud of in the entire mess.

There were a lot of Guild members who felt the same way I did, and our number increased with every vote. But we were never able to surmount the early emotional move against strikers. The majority opinion was to keep on working, and all but a handful of us went along with it. We walked back across the picket line, being spit on, punched and cursed. What hurt the most, however, was being called scabs for the first time in our lives.

Fifteen months later, I left Washington to come to Chicago. It was a strange parting, for I had enjoyed the way journalistic juices flow at the *Post* and the friendship of good and talented people. And yet I couldn't help thinking I had done wrong there, had sullied myself and needlessly hurt strangers in the process.

The doubt, the shame, the whatever-you-want-to-call-it is still with me as I watch the umpires picketing outside big-league ballparks. They have presented baseball with one of its rare moral dilemmas, and baseball has proven incapable of responding with the decency that is supposedly endemic to the game.

The fans are expected to believe that the umpires' life is a tolerable one, but umpires are on the road the entire season and their divorce rate is 60 per cent. The fans are expected to believe that the umps are asking for a huge pay increase, but all 52 of their salaries could be jumped 50 per cent for $300,000 less than Pete Rose will make this season. The fans are expected to believe that the umps have broken their union's five-year collective bargaining agreement, but a federal judge has ruled that the agreement isn't in effect until each of them has negotiated his own salary. The American and National leagues refuse to negotiate.

Players and public aren't supposed to think about that, of course. They are supposed to think "Kill the umpire!" in a different context than usual and fool themselves into believing that there has been no drop in quality with the hacks who are presently calling balls, strikes and outs.

How dumb do Bowie Kuhn, Lee MacPhail, Chub Feeney and the rest of those jackasses think everybody outside the executive suite is?

Maybe they could be jerked back to reality if the nation's labor unions called a one-day boycott on baseball. Or perhaps the players, knowing they will be the next to be jerked around, could all go golfing on a day when they are supposed to be working. The most effective tool, however, would be if the scab umpires would take stock of what they are doing, turn around and go back home.

These aren't poor men scrambling to make a buck. Rather, they are the epitome of comfortable middle-class society, and as such, they seem to have forgotten what a screwing the powers-that-be can deliver. Worse yet, they aren't very good at umpiring. There is no point in going into all the calls they have missed or in imagining how some large, berserk ballplayer might rearrange their limbs. They should just have the decency to blush and get out. If they do that, they will be spared the sight I used to know only too well when I looked in a mirror—the sight of a scab.

Appendix II: Southern Sports

Per Capita Participation in All High School Sports
(percent above or below national average)

North Carolina	− 56	Tennessee	− 28
Alabama	− 54	Virginia	− 28
Louisiana	− 50	Texas	− 3
Mississippi	− 49	Georgia	+ 2
Florida	− 48	Arkansas	+ 74
South Carolina	− 30		

Per Capita Participation in High School Football

Louisiana	− 40	Georgia	− 2
North Carolina	− 39	Tennessee	+ 3
Alabama	− 39	Virginia	+ 14
South Carolina	− 15	Arkansas	+ 41
Mississippi	− 8	Texas	+ 51
Florida	− 6		

Per Capita Participation in High School Basketball

Florida	− 84	South Carolina	− 19
Mississippi	− 64	Tennessee	+ 6
North Carolina	− 47	Texas	+ 7
Alabama	− 28	Georgia	+ 25
Louisiana	− 28	Arkansas	+ 147
Virginia	− 23		

Per Capita Participation in High School Baseball

Florida	− 40	Tennesssee	− 7
Louisiana	− 30	Texas	+ 7
Virginia	− 29	Arkansas	+ 9
North Carolina	− 28	South Carolina	+ 10

*Negligible.

| Mississippi | − 21 | Georgia | + 30 |
| Alabama | − 18 | | |

Per Capita Participation in High School Outdoor Track

Alabama	− 79	Mississippi	− 34
North Carolina	− 65	South Carolina	− 18
Louisiana	− 61	Georgia	− 14
Tennessee	− 45	Arkansas	+ 43
Virginia	− 43	Texas	+ 50
Florida	− 42		

Per Capita Participation in High School Cross Country

Texas	*	South Carolina	− 57
Mississippi	*	Virginia	− 54
Alabama	− 93	Louisiana	− 45
North Carolina	− 86	Arkansas	− 13
Tennessee	− 77	Georgia	+ 4
Florida	− 71		

Per Capita Participation in High School Wrestling

Texas	*	Florida	− 73
Mississippi	*	North Carolina	− 72
Arkansas	− 96	Tennessee	− 55
Louisiana	− 96	Georgia	− 54
Alabama	− 89	Virginia	− 37
South Carolina	− 84		

Per Capita Participation in High School Golf

Louisiana	− 89	Tennesssee	− 34
Alabama	− 63	Georgia	− 19
Virginia	− 59	Arkansas	− 17
South Carolina	− 54	Mississippi	+ 42
North Carolina	− 51	Texas	+ 84
Florida	− 44		

Per Capita Participation in High School Tennis

Louisiana	− 88	Mississippi	− 47
North Carolina	− 79	Georgia	− 34
Alabama	− 78	South Carolina	+ 5
Tennessee	− 50	Texas	+ 66
Virginia	− 49	Arkansas	+ 125
Florida	− 48		

*Negligible.

Per Capita Participation in High School Swimming

Tennessee	*	Arkansas	− 15
Mississippi	*	Florida	− 12
South Carolina	− 94	Alabama	+ 1
Virginia	− 94	Georgia	+ 45
Louisiana	− 88	Texas	+ 46
North Carolina	− 86		

Per Capita Participation in High School Gymnastics

Texas	*	Louisiana	− 89
Arkansas	*	North Carolina	− 79
Tennessee	*	Florida	− 59
North Carolina	*	South Carolina	− 55
Mississippi	*	Georgia	+ 92
Alabama	*		

Participation in Women's Intercollegiate Sports
(percent of schools offering)

	South	National
Basketball	57	73.5
Volleyball	61	69.5
Softball	11	43
Hockey	14	44
Bowling	14	17
Tennis	71	71
Archery	7	10
Swimming	21	39
Gymnastics	14	48
Track	18	32
Golf	32	30
Badminton	21	22
Others	4	19.5

Source: *A Geography of American Sport* by John J. Rooney.

*Negligible.

Footnotes

The Owners: Figures Don't Lie But Liars Can Figure

1. *Left Field: The F.A.N.S. Bulletin*, October 1978.
2. *Sports Illustrated*, June 18, 1979, p. 24.
3. *Sports Illustrated*, April 19, 1979, p. 98.
4. Plimpton, George, *One More July: A Football Dialogue with Bill Curry*, p. 100.
5. *Sports Illustrated*, May 2, 1978.

The Athletes: Without a Hot Bat, It's a Cold World

1. Hoffman, Anne Byrne, *Echoes from the Schoolyard*, p. 25.
2. *Sports Illustrated*, July 17, 1978, p. 51.
3. *1978 Baker League* (Philadelphia) *Yearbook*, p. 60.
4. Hoffman, *op. cit.*, pp. 13-14.
5. *Sports Illustrated,* August 27, 1979.
6. *Black Sports,* April 1978, p. 60.
7. *Sports Illustrated*, June 11, 1979, p. 36.
8. Rozin, Skip, *One Step From Glory: On the Fringe of Professional Sport*, p. 298.
9. *Ibid.*
10. Bradley, Bill, *Life on the Run*, p. 26.

The Fans: No Unemployed Need Apply

1. Kowet, Don, *The Rich Who Own Sports*, p. 95.
2. *Black Sports*, September 1977, p. 62.

3. *Sporting News*, April 22, 1978.

The Olympics: If the Shoe Fits, Sell It!

1. Johnson, William O., Jr., *All That Glitters Is Not Gold*, p. 176.
2. *Ibid.*, p. 177.
3. Edwards, Harry, *The Revolt of the Black Athlete*, p. 64.
4. *Track and Field News*, February 1980.
5. *Sport*, July 1979, p. 32.
6. *Sports Illustrated*, 1979.
7. Johnson, *op. cit.*, p. 81.
8. Chavoor, Sherman with Davidson, Bill, *The Fifty Meter Jungle*.
9. Johnson, *op. cit.*, p. 99.
10. *Track and Field News*, April 1979, p. 64.
11. *Sports Illustrated*, February 1979, p. 19.

The Locker Room is A Ghetto

1. *Basketball Times*, January 29, 1979.
2. *Sports Illustrated*, August 19, 1974
3. Chalk, Ocania, *Black College Sport*, p. 238.
4. Wagenheim, Kal, *Clemente!*, p. 91.
5. *Sporting News*, November 11, 1980.
6. *Basketball Times*, January 29, 1979.
7. Telander, Rick, *Heaven Is a Playground: The World of Inner-City Basketball*, p. 1.
8. *Sport*, December 1978, p. 42.
9. *Sport*, March 1979, p. 26.
10. *Basketball Times*, January 29, 1979.
11. Axthelm, Pete, *The City Game*, p. 79.
12. Bradley, Bill, *Life on the Run*, p. 72.
13. Axthelm, *op. cit.*, pp. 126–7.
14. Prokop, Dave, editor, *The African Running Revolution*, p. 68.
15. Plimpton, George, *One More July: A Football Dialogue with Bill Curry*, p. 86.

16. AP Wire Story, August 28, 1978.
17. *Sport*, August 1978.

Muhammad Ali

1. Libby, Bill, *Life in the Pit: The Deacon Jones Story*, p. 66.
2. Atyeo, Don and Dennis, Felix, *Holy Warrior: Muhammad Ali*, p. 51.
3. *Ibid.*, p. 15.
4. *Ibid.*, p. 52.
5. *Ibid.*, p. 53.
6. *Ibid.*, p. 61.
7. *Ibid.*, p. 62.
8. *Ibid.*, p. 63.
9. *Ibid.*, p. 72.
10. *Ibid.*, p. 68.
11. *Ibid.*, p. 66.
12. *Ibid.*, p. 71.

The Good, the Bad, and the Might-Have-Been

1. Wagenheim, Kal, *Clemente!*, p. 55.
2. *Ibid.*
3. *Ibid.*
4. *Ibid.*
5. Libby, Bill, *"King Richard": The Richard Petty Story*.
6. NBA Game Program, December 1978.
7. *Ibid.*
8. *Sports Illustrated*, May 28, 1979.
9. Vare, Robert, *Buckeye: A Study of Coach Woody Hayes and the Ohio State Football Machine*, p. 64.
10. *Ibid.*, p. 32.
11. *Ibid.*, p. 38.
12. *Ibid.*, p. 38.
13. *Sports Illustrated*, October 15, 1979.
14. *Sports Illustrated*, December 1978.
15. *Sport*.
16. *Sports Illustrated*, July 23, 1979.

17. *Sports Illustrated*, October 16, 1978.
18. *Ibid.*
19. *Ibid.*
20. *Ibid.*
21. *Ibid.*
22. *New Times*, October 16, 1978.
23. *Ibid.*
24. *Ibid.*

Three Times a Lady: Bench Press, Deadlift, Squat

1. Kaplan, Janice, *Women and Sports*, p. 69.
2. *In These Times*, June 27–July 3, 1979.
3. Petty, Jane R., *Almost as Fairly: The First Year of Title IX Implementation in Six Southern States*, p. 45.
4. *Women's Sports*, July 1980.
5. *Soul Magazine*, September 1979.
6. Petty, *op. cit.*, p. 55.

Recruit-Out on the Plantation: The Economics of College Sports

1. *Sports Illustrated*, September 1, 1980.
2. *Midwest Basketball News*, Vol. 1, No. 2, p. 3
3. Wire Service Story.
4. Roberts, Michael, *Fans: How We Go Crazy Over Sports*, p. 43.
5. Durso, Joseph and The New York Times Sports Department, *The Sports Factory: An Investigation into College Sports*, p. 57.
6. Denlinger, Kent and Shapiro, Len, *Athletes for Sale*, p. 215.
7. *Cleveland Plain Dealer*, January 6, 1979.
8. *Sports Illustrated*, September 10, 1979, p. 10.
9. Vare, Robert, *Buckeye: A Study of Coach Woody Hayes and the Ohio State Football Machine*, p. 94.
10. Shaw, Gary, *Meat on the Hoof*, p. 121.

Rules Are All Right If There's Someone Left to Play the Game: The Economics of High School Sports

1. *Proceedings of the National Federation's Seventh Annual National Conference of High School Directors of Athletics*, 1976.
2. *Newsweek*, September 5, 1977, p. 73.
3. Interscholastic Athletic Administration, Spring 1977.
4. *The Wall Street Journal*, February 28, 1980.

The Way Out

1. Petty, Jane R., *Almost as Fairly: The First Year of Title IX Implementation in Six Southern States*, p. 51.
2. Brown, Larry and Gildea, William, *I'll Always Get Up*.

Bibliography

Unknown to almost everyone, there is a tremendous reservoir of progressive sports literature in the United States. Some can be found in bookstores, more in libraries, but much more of it is out of print and hard to find.

But I can personally testify that the game is worth the hunt. This book exists only by standing on the shoulders of what has been written before. I urge the interested reader to delve into this treasure house of material. You cannot change something until you understand what it is.

Books

Amateur Athletic Union 1977 Directory. Indianapolis: AAU, 1977.

Amdur, Neil, *The Fifth Down.* New York: Coward, McCann & Geoghegan, Inc., 1971.

Angell, Roger, *Five Seasons: A Baseball Companion.* New York: Popular Library, 1978.

Atyeo, Don and Dennis, Felix, *Holy Warrior: Muhammad Ali.* New York: Simon and Schuster, 1975.

Axthelm, Pete, *The City Game.* New York: Harper & Row, 1970.

Baker League Yearbook. Philadelphia: 1978.

Basic Agreement Between the American League of Professional Baseball Clubs and the National League of Professional Baseball Clubs and Major League Baseball Players Association. 1976.

Berkow, Ira, *Beyond the Dream: Occasional Heroes of Sports.* New York: Atheneum, 1975.

Blount, Roy Jr., *About Three Bricks Shy of a Load.* Boston: Little, Brown & Company, 1974.

Bradley, Bill, *Life on the Run*. New York: Quadrangle Press, The New York Times Book Company, 1976.

Brown, Larry and Gildea, William, *I'll Always Get Up*. New York: Simon & Schuster, 1973.

Burman, George, editor, *Conference on the Economics of Professional Sport, Proceedings*. Washington: National Football League Players Association, 1974.

Chalk, Ocania, *Black College Sport*. New York: Dodd, Mead & Company, 1976.

———, *Pioneers of Black Sport*. New York: Dodd, Mead & Company, 1975.

Chavoor, Sherman with Davidson, Bill, *The 50 Meter Jungle*. New York: Coward, McCann & Geoghegan, 1973.

Colton, Larry, *Idol Time: Profile in Blazermania*. Forest Grove, OR: Timber Press, 1978.

Comite International Olympique, *Biographies Olympiques*. Lausanne, Switzerland: Chateau de Vidy, 1976.

Cosell, Howard, *Cosell*. Chicago: Playboy Press, 1973.

Cousy, Bob with Devaney, John, *The Killer Instinct*. New York: Random House, 1975.

Davis, Lance and Quirk, James, *The Ownership and Valuation of Professional Sports Franchises*. Pasadena, CA: California Institute of Technology, Division of the Humanities and Social Sciences, 1975.

———, *Tax Writeoffs and the Value of Sports Teams*. Pasadena, CA: California Institute of Technology, Division of the Humanities and Social Services, 1975.

Demmet, Henry G., *The Economics of Professional Team Sports*. Lexington, MA: Lexington Books, 1973.

Denlinger, Kent and Shapiro, Len, *Athletes For Sale*. New York: T.Y. Crowell, 1975.

DeVries, Herbert, *Physiology of Exercise,* Second Edition. Dubuque, IA: William C. Brown Company, 1974.

Dickey, Glenn, *Champs and Chumps: An Insider's Look at America's Sports Heroes*. San Francisco: Chronicle Books, 1976.

Gardner, Paul, *Nice Guys Finish Last: Sport and American Life*. New York: Universe Books, 1975.

Gilmer, J. Lance, *The Last Touchdown*. Los Angeles: Holloway House Publishing Company, 1978.

Gilmore, Al-Tony, *Bad Nigger! The National Impact of Jack Johnson*. Port Washington, NY: National University Publications, Kennikat Press, 1975.

Glader, Eugene A., *Amateurism and Athletics*. West Point, NY: Leisure Press, 1978.

Greenspan, Bud, *We Wuz Robbed*. New York: Grossett & Dunlap, 1976.

Henderson, Edwin B. and the Editors of *Sport* Magazine, *The Black Athlete: Emergence and Arrival*. New York: Publishers Company, Inc., 1968.

Hill, Art, *Don't Let Baseball Die*. AuTrain, Michigan: Avery Color Studios, 1978.

———, *I Don't Care If I Never Come Back*. New York: Simon & Schuster, 1980.

Hoch, Paul, *Rip Off the Big Game: The Exploitation of Sports by the Power Elite*. New York: Doubleday & Company, Inc., 1972.

Hoffman, Anne Byrne, *Echoes from the Schoolyard*. New York: Hawthorn Books, Inc., 1977.

Izenberg, Jerry, *How Many Miles to Camelot? The All-American Sport Myth*. New York: Holt, Reinhart & Winston, 1972.

Jackson, Phil and Rosen, Charles, *Maverick: More Than A Game*. Chicago: Playboy Press, 1975.

Johnson, Blaine, *What's Happening: A Revealing Journey Through the World of Professional Basketball*. Englewood Cliffs, NJ: Prentice-Hall, Inc., 1975.

Johnson, William O. Jr., *All That Glitters Is Not Gold*. New York: G. D. Putnam & Sons, 1972.

Jones, Wali and Washington, Jim, *Black Champions Challenge American Sports*. New York: D. McKay Company, 1972.

Jordan, Pat, *Black Coach*. New York: Dodd, Mead & Company, 1971.

———, *Chase the Game*. New York: Dodd, Mead & Company, 1979.

Kahn, Roger, *A Season in the Sun*. New York: Harper & Row, 1977.

Kanin, David, "The Role of Sport in International Relations" (Doctoral Thesis, Fletcher School of Law and Diplomacy) MA: Tufts University, 1976.

Kaplan, Janice *Women and Sports*. New York: The Viking Press, 1979.

Kowet, Don, *The Rich Who Own Sports*. New York: Random House, 1977.

Lapchick, Richard E., *The Politics of Race and International Sport: The Case of South Africa*. Westport, CN: Greenwood Press, 1975.

Lardner, Rex, *Ali*. New York: Grosset & Dunlap, Inc., 1978.

Law and Contemporary Problems—Athletics. (Vol. XXXVIII, No. 1) Durham, NC: Duke University School of Law, 1973.

Lekarska, Nadejda, *Essays and Studies on Olympic Problems*. Sofia, Bulgaria: Medicina and Fizcultura, 1973.

Libby, Bill, *"King Richard": The Richard Petty Story*. Garden City, NY: Doubleday & Company, 1977.

———, *Life in the Pit: The Deacon Jones Story*. Garden City, NY: Doubleday & Company, 1970.

———, *The Walton Gang*. New York: Coward, McCann & Geoghegan, 1974.

Lichtenstein, Grace, *A Long Way, Baby: Behind the Scenes in Women's Pro Tennis*. New York: William Morrow & Company, 1974.

Lipsyte, Robert, *Assignment: Sports*. New York: Harper & Row, 1970.

———, *Free To Be Muhammad Ali*. New York: Harper & Row, 1978.

———, *Sportsworld: An American Dreamland*. New York: The New York Times Book Company, Quadrangle, 1975.

Mandell, Arnold J., *The Nightmare Season*. New York: Random House, 1976.

McCallum, John D., *Ty Cobb*. New York: Praeger Publishers, 1975.

Michener, James A., *Sports in America*. New York: Random House, 1976.

National Hockey League, *NHL-NHLPA Collective Bargaining Agreement*. National Hockey League, 1967.

Noll, Roger G., editor, *Government and the Sports Business*. Washington, DC: The Brookings Institution, 1974.

Ogbu, John U., *Minority Education and Caste: The American System in Cross-Cultural Perspective*. New York: Academic Press, 1978.

Parrish, Bernie, *They Call It a Game*. New York: Dial Press, 1971.

Pepe, Phil, *Stand Tall: The Lew Alcindor Story.* New York: Grossett & Dunlap, 1970.

Petty, Jane R., *Almost as Fairly: The First Year of Title IX Implementation in Six Southern States.* Atlanta: Southeastern Public Education Program, 1977.

Plimpton, George, *One More July: A Football Dialogue with Bill Curry.* New York: Harper & Row, 1977.

President's Commission on Olympic Sports, *The Final Report of the President's Commission on Olympic Sports 1975-1977, Volume I.* Washington, DC: Government Printing Office, 1977.

————, *The Final Report of the President's Commission on Olympic Sports 1975-1977, Volume II.* Washington, DC: Government Printing Office, 1977.

Proceedings of the National Federation's Seventh Annual National Conference of High School Directors of Athletics. San Diego, CA: National Federation of State High School Associations, 1976.

Prokop, Dave, editor, *The African Running Revolution.* Mountain View, CA: World Publications, 1975.

Quirk, James, "An Economic Analysis of Team Movements in Professional Sports," (Reprinted from the *Symposium on Athletics*). Durham, NC: Duke University School of Law, 1973.

————, *Stadium Capacities and Attendance in Professional Sports.* Pasadena, CA: California Institute of Technology, Division of the Humanities and Social Sciences, 1975.

Rappoport, Ken, *Diamonds in the Rough.* New York: Grosset & Dunlap, 1979.

Reed, Willis and Pepe, Phil, *A View from the Rim: Willis Reed on Basketball.* Philadelphia: J. B. Lippincott Company, 1971.

Roberts, Michael. *Fans: How We Go Crazy Over Sports.* Washington, DC: The New Republic Book Company, Inc., 1976.

Robinson, Jackie. *I Never Had It Made.* Greenwich, CN: Fawcett Publications, Inc., 1972.

Rooney, John F. Jr., *A Geography of American Sport: From Cabin Creek to Anaheim.* Reading, MA: Addison-Wesley Publishing Company, 1974.

Roseboro, John and Libby, Bill, *Glory Days with the Dodgers.* New York: Atheneum, 1978.

Roundtable by the American Enterprise Institute for Public Policy Research, *Pro Sports: Should Government Intervene?* Washington, DC: American Enterprise Institute, 1977.

Rozin, Skip, *One Step From Glory: On the Fringe of Professional Sports*. New York: Simon & Schuster, 1979.

Rust, Art Jr., *"Get That Nigger Off the Field!": A Sparkling Informal History of the Black Man in Baseball*. New York: Delacorte Press, 1974.

Ryan, Bob, *The Pro Game: The World of Professional Basketball*. New York: McGraw-Hill Book Company, 1975.

Sample, Johnny, *Confessions of a Dirty Ballplayer*. New York: The Dial Press, 1970.

Schaap, Dick, editor, *Instant Replay: The Green Bay Diary of Jerry Kramer*. New York: The New American Library, Inc., 1969.

——, *Quarterbacks Have All the Fun*. Chicago: Playboy Press, 1974.

Schneider, Russell J., *Frank Robinson: The Making of a Manager*. New York: Coward, McCann & Geoghegan, 1976.

Scott, Jack, *The Athletic Revolution*. New York: The Free Press, 1971.

——, *Bill Walton: On the Road with the Portland Trail Blazers*. New York: Thomas Y. Crowell Publishers, 1976.

Scott, Thomas O., *Education Is Our Right: The Bakke Case and the Developing Crisis in Education*. Chicago: Equal Rights Congress, 1977.

Schecter, Leonard, *The Jocks*. New York: Paperback Library, 1970.

Shaw, Gary, *Meat on the Hoof: The Hidden World of Texas Football*. New York: St. Martin's Press, 1972.

Silverman, Al, editor, *The Best of Sport: 1946-71*. New York: The Viking Press, 1971.

Starr, Bill. *The Strongest Shall Survive: Strength Training for Football*. Fitness Products Limited, 1978.

Sugar, Bert, *"The Thrill of Victory": The Inside Story of ABC Sports*. New York: Hawthorn Books, Inc., 1978.

Talamini, John and Page, Charles, editors, *Sports & Society: An Anthology*. Boston: Little, Brown & Company, 1973.

Telander, Rick, *Heaven is a Playground: The World of Inner-City Basketball*. New York: Grosset & Dunlap, 1976.

Thomas, Vaughan, *Science & Sport: How to Measure and Improve Athletic Performance.* Boston: Little, Brown & Company, 1970.

Torres, Jose and Sugar, Bert, *Sting Like a Bee.* New York: Abelard-Schuman, 1971.

Turkin, Hy and Thompson, S.C., *The Official Encyclopedia of Baseball.* Garden City, NY: Doubleday & Company, Inc., 1977.

Twin, Stephanie, *Out of the Bleachers: Writings on Women and Sport.* New York: McGraw-Hill Book Company, 1979.

United States Olympic Committee, *Constitution, By-Laws, and General Rules.* New York: Olympic House, 1977.

Vare, Robert, *Buckeye: A Study of Coach Woody Hayes and the Ohio State Football Machine.* New York: Harper's Magazine Press, 1974.

Wagenheim, Kal, *Clemente!* New York: Washington Square Press, 1973.

Weinberg, Meyer. *A Chance to Learn: A History of Race and Education in the United States.* New York: Cambridge University Press, 1977.

West, Jerry with Libby, Bill, *Mr. Clutch: The Jerry West Story.* Englewood Cliffs, NJ: Prentice-Hall, Inc., 1969.

Winick, Matt, *National Basketball Association Official Guide.* St. Louis, MO: The Sporting News Publishing Company, 1978.

Wismer, Harry, *The Public Calls It Sport.* Englewood Cliffs, NJ: Prentice-Hall, Inc., 1965.

Wolf, David, *Foul!—The Connie Hawkins Story.* New York: Holt, Reinhart & Winston, 1972.

Woolf, Bob, *Behind Closed Doors: How Pro-Athletes Become Millionaires.* New York: The New American Library, Inc., 1976.

Journals, Magazines, and Newspapers

African Agenda
Agenda
American Journal of Sports Medicine
Arena Review
Arkansas Industrial Development Bulletin
Ball & Strikes: Official Newspaper of the Amateur Softball Association
Basketball Times
Basketball Weekly
Black Scholar
Black Sports
Boston Globe
Boxing Illustrated
Chicago Defender
Christian Science Monitor
Cleveland Plain Dealer
Denis Reno's New England and Region F Weightlifters' Newsletter
Ebony
Education, USA
El Cuhamil
Gymnastics News
Integrated Education
International Olympic Lifter
International Review of Sports Sociology
Interscholastic Athletic Administration
Iron Man
Jet
Journal of Sport and Social Issues
JUCO Review
Los Angeles Times
Left Field: The F.A.N.S. Bulletin
Mountain Journal
Muscular Development

Navajo Times
NCAA Statistics Service Bulletin
Newsweek
New York Times
Physical Educator
Players
Powerlifting USA
Referee
Ring
Rodeo News
Rolling Stone
Runners World
Sepia
South African Boxing World
Sport
Sport Sociology Bulletin
Sports Illustrated
Strength and Health
The Blue Chips
The Runner
The Sporting News
Time
Track and Field News
TV Guide
Wall Street Journal
Women's Sports